CHECKING CHINA'S MARITIME PUSH

HEARING

BEFORE THE

SUBCOMMITTEE ON ASIA AND THE PACIFIC

OF THE

COMMITTEE ON FOREIGN AFFAIRS
HOUSE OF REPRESENTATIVES

ONE HUNDRED FIFTEENTH CONGRESS

FIRST SESSION

FEBRUARY 28, 2017

Serial No. 115–6

Printed for the use of the Committee on Foreign Affairs

Available via the World Wide Web: http://www.foreignaffairs.house.gov/ or
http://www.gpo.gov/fdsys/

U.S. GOVERNMENT PUBLISHING OFFICE

24–444PDF   WASHINGTON : 2017

For sale by the Superintendent of Documents, U.S. Government Publishing Office
Internet: bookstore.gpo.gov   Phone: toll free (866) 512–1800; DC area (202) 512–1800
Fax: (202) 512–2104   Mail: Stop IDCC, Washington, DC 20402–0001

COMMITTEE ON FOREIGN AFFAIRS

EDWARD R. ROYCE, California, *Chairman*

CHRISTOPHER H. SMITH, New Jersey
ILEANA ROS-LEHTINEN, Florida
DANA ROHRABACHER, California
STEVE CHABOT, Ohio
JOE WILSON, South Carolina
MICHAEL T. McCAUL, Texas
TED POE, Texas
DARRELL E. ISSA, California
TOM MARINO, Pennsylvania
JEFF DUNCAN, South Carolina
MO BROOKS, Alabama
PAUL COOK, California
SCOTT PERRY, Pennsylvania
RON DeSANTIS, Florida
MARK MEADOWS, North Carolina
TED S. YOHO, Florida
ADAM KINZINGER, Illinois
LEE M. ZELDIN, New York
DANIEL M. DONOVAN, JR., New York
F. JAMES SENSENBRENNER, JR.,
    Wisconsin
ANN WAGNER, Missouri
BRIAN J. MAST, Florida
FRANCIS ROONEY, Florida
BRIAN K. FITZPATRICK, Pennsylvania
THOMAS A. GARRETT, JR., Virginia

ELIOT L. ENGEL, New York
BRAD SHERMAN, California
GREGORY W. MEEKS, New York
ALBIO SIRES, New Jersey
GERALD E. CONNOLLY, Virginia
THEODORE E. DEUTCH, Florida
KAREN BASS, California
WILLIAM R. KEATING, Massachusetts
DAVID N. CICILLINE, Rhode Island
AMI BERA, California
LOIS FRANKEL, Florida
TULSI GABBARD, Hawaii
JOAQUIN CASTRO, Texas
ROBIN L. KELLY, Illinois
BRENDAN F. BOYLE, Pennsylvania
DINA TITUS, Nevada
NORMA J. TORRES, California
BRADLEY SCOTT SCHNEIDER, Illinois
THOMAS R. SUOZZI, New York
ADRIANO ESPAILLAT, New York
TED LIEU, California

AMY PORTER, *Chief of Staff* THOMAS SHEEHY, *Staff Director*

JASON STEINBAUM, *Democratic Staff Director*

SUBCOMMITTEE ON ASIA AND THE PACIFIC

TED S. YOHO, Florida, *Chairman*

DANA ROHRABACHER, California
STEVE CHABOT, Ohio
TOM MARINO, Pennsylvania
MO BROOKS, Alabama
SCOTT PERRY, Pennsylvania
ADAM KINZINGER, Illinois
ANN WAGNER, Missouri

BRAD SHERMAN, California
AMI BERA, California
DINA TITUS, Nevada
GERALD E. CONNOLLY, Virginia
THEODORE E. DEUTCH, Florida
TULSI GABBARD, Hawaii

(II)

CONTENTS

CHECKING CHINA'S MARITIME PUSH

TUESDAY, FEBRUARY 28, 2017

HOUSE OF REPRESENTATIVES,
SUBCOMMITTEE ON ASIA AND THE PACIFIC,
COMMITTEE ON FOREIGN AFFAIRS,
Washington, DC.

The subcommittee met, pursuant to notice, at 2:30 p.m., in room 2172, Rayburn House Office Building, Hon. Ted Yoho (chairman of the subcommittee) presiding.

Mr. YOHO. We are going to call this meeting to order. This will be the first committee hearing of the Asia and the Pacific Subcommittee, and it is an honor to be the chairman.

I welcome you guys here, and thank you for being part of this committee and allowing me to be at the helm of it.

Good afternoon and welcome to the first meeting of the Subcommittee on Asia and the Pacific of the 115th Congress. The subcommittee will come to order. Members present will be permitted to submit written statements to be included in the official hearing. Without objection, the hearing record will remain open for 5 calendar days to allow statements, questions, extraneous material for the record subject to length limitations in the rules.

The People's Republic of China's aggressive and provocative behavior in the maritime territorial disputes represents a threat to vital U.S. interests as severe as those from Russia, Iran, North Korea, and terrorism from the Middle East, according to the Heritage Foundation's 2017 index for U.S. military strength. Since 2013, China has rapidly advanced its maritime capabilities, employed them to transform the South China Sea with artificial islands, place Japan under increasing pressure in the East China Sea, and attempt to restrict freedom of navigation in its near waters. Unbelievably, China has suffered little, if any, cost for this maritime push.

In the South China Sea, China has built over 3,200 acres of land over disputed features in the Spratly Islands, complete with military-capable airstrips, ports, radars, anti-aircraft weapons, and, confirmed just last week, surface-to-air missile silos.

China also continues to press Japanese vessels around the Senkaku Islands in the East China Sea. Uncommitted to existing global norms, China continually undermines attempts at a unified response of these activities from ASEAN and has attempted to use its economic influence to buy off other claimants.

The United States and our allies and partners recognize that our military presence in the Western Pacific has been a force for stability and for good across decades, but so far, we haven't acted with nearly the level of resolve that China has in its aggressive pursuit of its arbitrary claims.

For example, officials from the last administration proclaimed the importance of freedom of navigation far and wide in response to China's effort to restrict it. But this fundamental right, and the international law which protects it, was only hesitantly enforced with four Freedom of Navigation operations, none of which challenged China's tacit assertion that its artificial islands are entitled to territorial seas.

For nearly a decade, we have said much and done little. While the South and East China Seas may seem distant, we have important national interests at stake. The disputed areas are key global economic and trade arteries. Nearly 30 percent of the world's maritime trade moves through the area. Domination of these routes might allow a regional power to use disruption as leverage.

The security of these areas is also essential for the energy security of key U.S. defense allies and partners. Most of the energy supplied to South Korea, Japan, and Taiwan comes through the South China Sea. Energy insecurity among our friends in the region could have serious implications for our ability to handle potential contingencies arising from North Korea and elsewhere.

Perhaps most importantly, the lack of U.S. resolve hasn't just allowed China to change the status quo on the ground but contributes to worries among our allies and partners that the United States lacks sufficient commitment to the region and feeds the narrative that China has been successful in degrading U.S. influence and global norms. The perceived potency of our military and diplomatic power is very much at risk. The South and East China Seas are strategic keys to East Asia, and acquiescence to restrictions on U.S. Forces' freedom of operations there will undermine the U.S. security guarantee and degrade both regional and world stability.

We need a new strategy, and the entrance of a new administration represents a good opportunity to form and implement better policies to represent or reassert U.S. strengths in these critical areas. It may be time to consider an assertive plan. As we have seen, endlessly backing away from conflicts carries its own risks. China has taken advantage of U.S. acquiescence to revise the status quo, advancing its strategic interests in ways that raise the risk of conflict. Timidity hasn't de-escalated these maritime disputes; it has only raised the stakes.

Today, we will hear suggestions from our expert panel for defining U.S. goals and addressing China's maritime push as well as policy options to operationalize more effective U.S. engagement on this important issue.

At this moment, without objection, the witnesses' written statements will be entered into the hearing record.

I now turn to our ranking member, Mr. Sherman, for any remarks he may have.

[The prepared statement of Mr. Yoho follows:]

Opening Statement of the Honorable **Ted Yoho (R-FL)**
Chairman of the Subcommittee on Asia and the Pacific
Subcommittee Hearing: Checking China's Maritime Push
February 28, 2017

(As prepared for delivery)

The People's Republic of China's aggressive and provocative behavior in maritime territorial disputes represents a threat to vital U.S. interests as severe as those from Russia, Iran, North Korea, and terrorism from the Middle East, according to the Heritage Foundation's 2017 Index of U.S. Military Strength. Since 2013, China has rapidly advanced its maritime capabilities and employed them to transform the South China Sea with artificial islands, place Japan under increasing pressure in the East China Sea, and attempt to restrict freedoms of navigation in its near waters. Unbelievably, China has suffered little if any cost for this maritime push.

In the South China Sea, China has built over 3,200 acres of land over disputed features in the Spratly Islands, complete with military-capable airstrips, ports, radars, and antiaircraft weapons. Just last week, satellite imagery confirmed that China has installed surface-to-air missile silos on its artificial islands on Subi, Mischief, and Fiery Cross reefs. China also continues to press the Japan Coast Guard, the Maritime Self-Defense Force, and the Air Self-Defense Force around the Japanese-administered Senkaku Islands in the East China Sea. Uncommitted to existing global norms, China continually undermines attempts at a unified response to these activities from ASEAN and has attempted to use its economic influence to buy off other claimants.

The United States and our allies and partners recognize that our military presence in the Western Pacific has been a force for stability and for good across decades. But so far, we haven't acted with nearly the level of resolve that China has in its aggressive pursuit of its arbitrary claims. For example, officials from the last administration proclaimed the importance of freedom of navigation far and wide in response to China's efforts to restrict it. But this fundamental right, and the international law which protects it, was only hesitantly enforced with four freedom of navigation operations, none of which challenged China's tacit assertion that its artificial islands are entitled to territorial seas.

For nearly a decade, we have said much, and done little. While the South and East China Seas may seem distant, we have important national interests at stake. The disputed areas are key global economic and trade arteries. Nearly 30 percent of the world's maritime trade moves through the area. Domination of these routes might allow a regional power to use disruption as leverage.

The security of these areas is also essential for the energy security of key U.S. defense allies and partners. Most of the energy supplies of South Korea, Japan, and Taiwan come through the South

China Sea. Energy insecurity among our friends in the region could have serious implications for our ability to handle potential contingencies arising from North Korea and elsewhere.

Perhaps most importantly, the lack of U.S. resolve hasn't just allowed China to change the status quo on the ground, but contributes to worries among our allies and partners that the United States lacks sufficient commitment to the region, and feeds the narrative that China has been successful in degrading U.S. influence and global norms. The perceived potency of our military and diplomatic power is very much at risk. The South and East China Seas are strategic keys to East Asia, and acquiescence to restrictions on U.S. forces' freedom of operations there will undermine the U.S. security guarantee and degrade both regional and world stability.

We need a new strategy, and the entrance of the new administration represents a good opportunity to form and implement better policies to reassert U.S. strength in these critical areas. It may be time to consider a more assertive plan. As we have seen, endlessly backing away from conflict carries its own risks. China has taken advantage of U.S. acquiescence to revise the status quo, advancing its strategic interests in ways that raise the risk of conflict. Timidity hasn't de-escalated these maritime disputes; it has only raised the stakes.

Today, we will hear suggestions from our expert panel for defining U.S. goals in addressing China's maritime territorial aggression, as well as policy options to operationalize more effective U.S. engagement on this important issue.

Mr. SHERMAN. Chairman Yoho, thanks for those remarks. Welcome to your new role. I look forward to working with you. And you will find, as you already know, that I am hawkish on our trade relationship with China and dovish on the so-called islands, more reefs than anything else.

China is waging—every day—an attack on American working families by refusing to accept our exports and by demanding co-production agreements when they will take a few of our exports, demanding that we transfer factories and technology as a price for having some limited access to their markets. That is devastating State after State in America. And, instead, we are focused on these islands.

Why? Well, because the most powerful economic decision maker in America is Wall Street, and they want us to ignore the devastation of America's working families. And the most important decisionmaker in the area of our military and national security is the Pentagon and others who want to see a 10-percent increase in our defense budget, and they know that China is the only worthy adversary to the might of the American military.

So I do think it is important that we look at our bilateral relations with China, and the aggression of China in the South China Sea, the East China Sea, is an irritant and maritime disputes and our support for a free, international maritime regime is important.

If it was more important, we might join UNCLOS and actually be part of the international order when it comes to maritime disputes. Instead, we focus all of our attention on China's refusal to adhere to international law on these disputes.

There are 20 maritime disputes that do not involve China, and not a single one of them has been the subject or even a partial subject of any hearing of this subcommittee, any subcommittee, or the full committee of Foreign Affairs. Why? Because none of those disputes justify a massive increase in the American military budget, and none of those disputes distract us sufficiently from the war that China is waging against American working families.

Now, we are told that these ports—these islands pose this great threat to international trade because $5 trillion of trade goes close to these islands or reefs. Yet, almost all of that trade is going in and out of Chinese ports, and if China controlled these reefs, they could blockade their own ports, and what threat, witnesses, does that pose to American national security?

Now a few—some of that trade—are oil tankers coming from Saudi Arabia to Japan, and in a worst-case scenario—and I do note—that if China somehow dominated wrongfully and tried to interdict in this area, those tankers would have to change their course, thus increasing the cost of gasoline in Japan by at least $1/10$ of 1 cent per gallon. That is the worst that could happen to international trade. If they could blockade their own ports, they could force some trade to go a little—on a slightly different route. And that is a level of aggression that I don't think any of us would tolerate.

So we have—let me see.

Finally, we have got to look at burden sharing. Japan demands that we risk lives to defend these uninhabited islands and that we spend billions—and apparently need to shut down a quarter or a third of our State Department to be able to afford to do it—to defend these islands. They spend less than 1 percent of their GDP on defense. We have to defend their islands. There is no oil there, but if there is any oil there, it is Japan's oil or South Korea's oil; it is not our oil. But, also, what happens to our mutual defense treaty when America was attacked on 9/11? Our European forces—partners at least put troops in harm's way. Some of them are spending 2 percent of their GDP on defense. Japan said, "Well, we have got this constitution. So we won't help you, and we won't amend our constitution either to help you." So Americans died by the thousands, a country with a mutual defense treaty with the United States binding them to help defend us, basically ignored. I think there was a ship in the Indian Ocean that had a Japanese flag on it.

So we are told that the Pentagon needs more money to defend islands that Japan is unwilling to tax itself to defend, a country that responded rather insufficiently when America was attacked.

And we are told: Don't pay attention to China's attack on American working families; pay only attention to whether they are adding a little dirt to a reef in the South China Sea.

I yield back.

Mr. YOHO. I appreciate my colleague's comments there. And, yes, there are a lot of other conflicts or areas that are a concern out there. But when we start seeing military equipment going in their land strips and things like that, I think it causes more concern in this issue. And I look forward to the dialogue.

And at this point, I would like to yield a minute to my colleague Mr. Rohrabacher from California.

Mr. ROHRABACHER. And congratulations, Mr. Chairman——

Mr. YOHO. Thank you.

Mr. ROHRABACHER [continuing]. On being Mr. Chairman.

Let's just note that President Abe in Japan has been doing his best to end the type of relationship that you have just described. President Abe and the people of Japan are honorable people, and they are courageous people when they have to defend their interests. We have been doing that, and we have insisted upon that since the end of the Second World War.

President Abe is moving forward now and trying to move through his Parliament an end to the restrictions that were placed on Japan by their constitution after the Second World War.

I think that President—and we should applaud that. I don't know if—certainly, the last administration did not applaud it, and I would hope that President Trump would, indeed, look at what Abe is trying to do to become an equal partner rather than a junior partner who is being taken care of. So we should applaud that.

And, second of all, in terms of what is going on with the Chinese, if we turn our back and just say, "That doesn't affect us," what we are talking about is an arrogant disruption of international rights-of-way both in the air and on the sea that will do nothing but embolden this rotten dictatorship in Beijing from moving forward with even more aggressive moves elsewhere.

Mr. YOHO. Thank you.

Now we will turn to Mr. Bera, Dr. Bera, from California.

Mr. BERA. Thank you. I want to add my congratulations to Chairman Yoho.

Mr. YOHO. Thank you.

Mr. BERA. And welcome back to the ranking member.

I think this is a timely topic for us to start this session of Congress off and this subcommittee off. I was in Japan last week, had a chance to meet with the Prime Minister, Prime Minister Abe, and some of his team, and I think it is very important for us to reassure our allies in the region that we will uphold our commitments. I mean, we can talk about the South China Sea. We can talk about the East China Sea. And more acutely what is happening in North Korea is an existential threat to Japan and our allies in the Republic of Korea. So this is very much a timely topic.

And I would agree with my colleague from California, Mr. Rohrabacher, that Prime Minister Abe is trying to step up some of Japan's defensive capabilities, and they are working within the confines of their constitution to take on some more of the burden.

But, again, it was a bipartisan group meeting with our Japanese counterparts. We did send a strong message that we are ready to stand with our allies in the region in a collaborative way.

With that, I will yield back.

Mr. YOHO. Thank you. And I appreciate your comments.

And the thing that I am excited about is so much trade goes through here. This region is so important to so many people around the world that it is having these discussions in the open that we can help maybe draft policies that would direct our State Department, our administration, and build alliances stronger in that area and focus on economies, trade, and national security that affects all of us. And so I look forward to those debates.

As typical for meetings, we will have 5 minutes of questioning. You will each have an opening statement of 5 minutes that will be submitted into the record. And then each member will go back and forth for 5 minutes of questioning.

And so, with that, I would like to introduce our panel.

Mr. Dean Cheng, senior research fellow at the Heritage Foundation's Asia Studies Center. Thank you. You have been here before, and we appreciate you coming back.

Dr. Michael Auslin, resident scholar and director of Japan studies at the American Enterprise Institute. And, again, we thank you for your contributions.

And Dr. Michael Swaine, senior fellow with the Carnegie Endowment for International Peace, Asia Program.

And I have read all of your opening statements and several things from you, Dr. Swaine, and I look forward to an informative hearing.

So, with that, Mr. Cheng, if you would start your opening statement. Thank you.

Mr. CHENG. Chairman Yoho.

Mr. YOHO. And make sure everybody turns their mike on when you speak.

STATEMENT OF MR. DEAN CHENG, SENIOR RESEARCH FELLOW, ASIAN STUDIES CENTER, THE HERITAGE FOUNDATION

Mr. CHENG. Chairman Yoho, Ranking Member Sherman, and members of the committee, thank you very much for the opportunity to testify before you this afternoon at the first meeting of the Asia and the Pacific Subcommittee. My name is Dean Cheng. I am the senior research fellow for Chinese political and security affairs at the Heritage Foundation, but my comments today reflect solely my own opinion and do not reflect the views necessarily of the Heritage Foundation.

As has been very clear to anyone who has been watching the news, China is heavily engaged in the South China Sea region as the PRC has been asserting claims over an extensive expanse of the South China Sea based on a combination of claims of historic rights and a so-called nine-dash line that was laid down in 1947 under the previous Government of the Republic of China.

The Permanent Court of Arbitration at the Hague, however, found that neither of those arguments was, in fact, a basis for legitimating China's very expansive claims, including its artificial island construction in the Spratlys.

It is worth, I think, considering a bit about why China is so interested in the South China Sea. And I would suggest that there are several factors involved that are driving China's insistence on pushing in the region, even when it antagonizes its neighbors. And these broadly fall into the categories of resources, strategic depth, and national reputation, as well as the potential capacity for the Chinese concept of deterrence, which it is important to note, for the Chinese incorporates the idea of coercion. If you all have read Bernard Brodie, Thomas Schelling, and Herman Kahn, the American concept of deterrence is solely focused on dissuasion, but for the Chinese, it incorporates coercion.

When we talk about resources in the South China Sea, we tend to assume that it is about oil. The funny thing is that, although there have been a number of studies about potential hydrocarbon reserves in the South China Sea, the actual amount of hydrocarbon discovered by various test walls has, in fact, been extremely limited. It hasn't yet panned out.

The main resource, currently, that is actually of particular interest to the Chinese but also to neighboring states is that of food. The South China Sea includes some of the richest fishing grounds in the world. And while some of those rich fishing grounds are actually now being pushed toward collapse due to overfishing, it nonetheless remains a key source of relatively free protein. As China moves up the socioeconomic scale, its people are demanding more protein. So, if you are going to try to meet those demands, you can import meat, which is going to be very expensive, or you can try to catch more of it basically off the hooks, so to speak.

The second aspect here is strategic depth. And here, the Chinese have a distinct need to control the East Asia littoral, not just the South China Sea but the waters up through the entire first island chain, as a defensive measure because China's center of gravity, its economic center of gravity, is now on the coast. If you think about Shenzhen, Shanghai, Pudong, Tianjin, these are all port cities, and this is what China has invested billions and billions of dollars over the last 30 years in terms of building up its economic infrastructure.

The South China Sea, however, is especially important given the militarization of Hainan Island, which contains, among other things, China's newest and largest space sport, a facility for ballistic missile submarines, a carrier berth, submarine pens, and multiple military airfields, including the one that the U.S. EP-3 had to crash land on after the collision in 2001.

One of the American trump cards is our submarines, our nuclear attack submarines. They are extremely quiet. China has openly discussed the creation of sonar surveillance arrays in the bottom of the South China Sea. Those arrays need to come up at some point in order to collect the data, to allow the data to be analyzed and exported. And I would suggest that some of these islands may serve that particular function.

In addition, for this Chinese Communist Party, legitimacy rests upon core interests. And among the core interests that were defined by the senior counselor Cui Tiankai in his meetings with then Secretary of State Clinton is maintaining territorial integrity and State sovereignty, which is especially important in the wake of the so-called century of humiliation that China suffered when China was faced with the potential of dismemberment.

So the South China Sea, like Taiwan, like Xinjiang, like Tibet, is increasingly associated by the Chinese leadership as, basically, if we lose this, where will it end? Where will it stop?

It is no surprise, then, that the U.S. has been accused of fomenting the entire South China Sea problem from the—by such senior leaders of General Fang Fenghui in his joint press conference with then Chairman of the Joint Chiefs Dempsey and Madam Fu Ying of the National People's Congress.

So, within this focus, within this broad context, then, China is driven by a number of considerations here to push for extending its sovereignty over what normally would be considered international common spaces. And this is likely to become even more urgent as China's leadership faces the 19th Party Congress this fall, where Xi Jinping is going to wind up with an entirely new leadership cadre.

In order to counter China, I think some of the things that we should be considering and which I hope the committee will consider future hearings are the issues of maintaining a presence in the region, emphasizing the legality of the Permanent Court of Arbitration's findings, and employing economic as well as more traditional political and diplomatic means to pressure China.

Thank you very much.

[The prepared statement of Mr. Cheng follows:]

The
Heritage Foundation

CONGRESSIONAL TESTIMONY

China's "Core" Maritime Interests:
Security and Economic Factors
Testimony before the Subcommittee on Asia

Committee on Foreign Affairs

U.S. House of Representatives

February 28, 2017

Dean Cheng
Senior Research Fellow, Asian Studies Center
The Heritage Foundation

Chairman Yoho, Ranking Member Sherman, and members of the House Foreign Affairs Committee. Thank you for the opportunity to testify to you this afternoon.

The South China Sea is a vital part of the global trading system. It is the carotid artery of international trade, through which some $5.3 trillion passes every year. Ships bound for Japan, South Korea, and Taiwan, as well as China, transit these waters, bearing imports to these nations and carrying exports to global markets.

Arguments that merchant shipping can avoid the South China Sea, such as by transiting to the east of the Philippines, fail to recognize the realities of modern shipping. Container ships run more like railways or airlines, with comparable margins in terms of time in port (down-time). It is no more acceptable to add a day to a ship's transit time than it would be to add a day to a train schedule or an airplane flight.

Consequently, increased tensions in the South China Sea will generate repercussions that will be felt not only regionally but globally, in terms of economic impacts. As important, how various nations behave with regards to this vital maritime crossroads will influence perceptions of strength, affect the applicability of the rule of international law, and ultimately shape regional security dynamics.

China Increasingly Depends on the Sea

As noted in previous testimony before this Committee and Subcommittee, the People's Republic of China (PRC) has become increasingly focused upon the maritime realm for both economic and national security reasons.

China depends upon access to the world's oceans in order to import the raw materials and energy which feed its industries, as well as the good which feeds its population. Indeed, since 2014, the PRC has been the world's largest net importer of petroleum.[1] In 2016, despite a slowing economy, Chinese oil imports reached 8 million barrels per day,[2] While some of this is shipped via rail and pipelines, most is transported by sea.

China is also now a net importer of key agricultural products, including wheat, barley, sorghum—and rice.[3] In addition, China imports substantial quantities of soybeans and oilseeds, as well as fats and oils. Although China produces most of its own meat and dairy products, the U.S. Department of Agriculture notes that there is an increasing reliance on imports in this sector as well. Indeed, a January

214 Massachusetts Avenue, NE • Washington, DC 20002 • (202) 546-4400 • heritage.org

31, 2017 update from the Department of Agriculture notes that "China has emerged as the world's leading agricultural importer and now officials in China are adjusting policies to accommodate the country's new status as an agricultural importer."[4]

Chinese National Security Is Increasingly Tied to the Sea

This growing dependence on the sea makes maritime concerns an essential part of Chinese national security calculations. This is exacerbated by China's increased vulnerability to seaborne threats. Under Mao Zedong, the Chinese leadership poured billions of dollars into developing the "third front" of defense industries, locating military industries deep in the Chinese interior (e.g., Shaanxi, Ningxia, and Sichuan provinces). The goal was to provide millions of square miles of territory (and potential defenses) to shield them from possible attack from either the United States or the Soviet Union.[5]

By contrast, China's economic center of gravity since the rise of Deng Xiaoping in the 1980s has been largely located on the coast. This has allowed such economic centers as Shenzhen, Shanghai, and Guangzhou to more easily access global trade routes for both imports of raw materials and exports of products. This has meant, however, that China's recent economic development is also more vulnerable to potential attack from the sea.

Chinese leaders have therefore made clear that maritime concerns are increasingly part of China's fundamental interests. State Councilor Dai Bingguo, in 2009, stated that China would maintain our core interests. And for China, our concern is we must uphold our basic systems, our national security; and secondly, the sovereignty and territorial integrity; and thirdly, economic and social sustained development.[6]

Those core interests include maritime concerns. Sovereignty and territorial integrity pertains not only to land features but maritime ones as well. Indeed, the Chinese have termed their maritime claims as "blue soil," underscoring their importance.[7]

Chinese leader Xi Jinping himself has linked maritime interests and core interests. In July 2013, Xi stated to a Politburo study session that while China would pursue the path of peaceful development, it would "never abandon its legitimate maritime rights and interests, and furthermore, it will never sacrifice its core national interests."[8] The importance of the maritime domain to Chinese national security was further emphasized when it was included in the 2015 National Security Law.[9]

It is clear that the Chinese leadership sees maritime affairs as a central part of the national interest. In order to secure those interests, Beijing is intent upon extending the reach of Chinese sovereignty, and to brook no opposition or challenge to that sovereignty. In this regard, Chinese behavior at sea parallels their efforts in other international common spaces. China is striving to compel others to accept its version of rules and behavior in adjacent waters, much as it is intent upon getting others to accept its rules and behavior in cyber space.

1. U.S. Energy Information Administration, "China," May 14, 2015, http://www.eia.gov/beta/international/analysis_includes/countries_long/China/china.pdf (accessed February 24, 2017).

2. Jenny W. Hsu, "Despite Slowdown, China's Oil Imports Surge," Marketwatch, March 7, 2016, http://www.marketwatch.com/story/despite-slowdown-chinas-oil-imports-surge-2016-03-07 (accessed February 24, 2017).

3. Fred Gale, James Hansen, and Michael Jewison, *China's Growing Demand for Agricultural Imports*, U.S. Department of Agriculture, Economic Research Service, Economic Information Bulletin #136 (February 2015), p. 9, https://www.ers.usda.gov/webdocs/publications/eib136/51888_eib136_summary.pdf (accessed February 24, 2017).

4. U.S. Department of Agriculture, Economic Research Service, "China: Overview," January 31, 2017, https://www.ers.usda.gov/topics/international-markets-trade/countries-regions/china/ (accessed February 24, 2017).

5. Barry Naughton, "The Third Front: Defence Industrialization in Chinese Interior," *The China Quarterly*, Vol. 115 (September, 1988).

6. Hillary Clinton, Timothy Geitner, Dai Bingguo, and Wang Qishan, "Closing Remarks for US-China Strategic and Economic Dialogue," July 28, 2009, http://www.state.gov/secretary/20092013clinton/rm/2009a/july/126599.htm (accessed February 24, 2017).

7. State Oceanic Administration, Ocean Development Strategy Research Study Group, *China's Ocean Development Report, 2010* (Beijing, PRC: Maritime Publishing House, 2010), p. 469.

8. "Xi Jinping at 8th CCP Politburo Study Session Emphasizes Attention to Maritime Affairs, Advancing Maritime Knowledge, Economic and Strategic Importance of the Maritime Domain, and Constantly Pushing Construction of a Strong Maritime Nation," *People's Daily*, August 1, 2013, http://paper.people.com.cn/rmrb/html/2013-08/01/nw.D110000renmrb_20130801_2-01.htm (accessed February 24, 2017).

9. National Security Law of the People's Republic of China, July 1, 2015, http://chinalawtranslate.com/2015nsl/?lang=en (accessed February 24, 2017).

In order to preserve those interests, it has become increasingly clear that China is prepared to challenge various international norms and rules, as it strives to extend its sovereignty over what others would consider international common spaces. When the Philippines brought a case before the Permanent Court of Arbitration (PCA) at the Hague, as provided for under the UN Convention on the Law of the Sea (UNCLOS), China chose not to participate in the proceedings. Beijing has subsequently chosen to ignore the findings of the PCA. Instead, it has continued to expand the infrastructure on the artificial islands it has built in the Spratly islands grouping, and is now building what appear to be military facilities. It is doing so in the face of the findings of the PCA that this activity has aggravated the dispute, and in the case of one feature—Mischief Reef—violating sovereign rights of the Philippines.

As important, it is steadily increasing regional tensions, as China's Southeast Asian neighbors increase their own defense capabilities, in part in order to counter Chinese actions. More worrisome, if Chinese efforts in the South China Sea are not met with a firm response, it is likely to apply the lessons learned to other disputes such as those with Japan over the Senkakus.

Growing Chinese Assertiveness in the South China Sea

As Naval War College professor Peter Dutton outlined in 2011, the disputes in the South China Sea actually cover three different aspects. First, there are disputes over sovereignty—who actually owns various features. Second is the related issue of jurisdiction—who administers the waters and airspace of related claimed Exclusive Economic Zones (EEZ), if anyone. Third, there is the issue of control—the right to conduct freedom of navigation and other military activities in various waters and airspace.[10]

Chinese claims to the South China Sea are encompassed within a nine-dash line (now ten dashes), which is in turn based upon maps issued by the Nationalist government. Unfortunately, the precise meaning of this nine-dash line has not been clarified by the PRC government. In particular, does the line indicate that all of the waters (and attendant airspace) belong to China?

Archival research in the files of the ROC government on Taiwan has led several scholars to suggest that the line was intended to encompass only the land features and immediately adjacent waters within it, and was **not** intended as a claim over the waters and airspace beyond those land features.[11] Some Chinese scholars recognize this argument. In 2014, Dr. Wu Shichun stated that "China has never claimed all waters in the U-shaped line. From the historical archives from Taiwan and China, it's clear that the line shows ownership of insular features within the U-shaped line."[12]

Unfortunately, the PRC government has not clarified whether this is *its* interpretation of the nine-dash line, nor has it indicated the precise nature of its claims. What it has done, through the construction of artificial islands, is attempt to change the facts on the ground (or in the water). It has therefore simultaneously claimed sovereignty, and has also claimed jurisdiction over an expansive exclusive economic zone. At the same time, by interfering with American naval operations as with the USNS *Impeccable* and USS *John McCain* in 2009 and the USS *Cowpens* in 2013, as well as dangerous approaches to U.S. patrol aircraft operating in the area, China is clearly acting as though it has control over these waters and airspace. It makes this argument, in turn, based upon its claims of sovereignty over this air and water space.

The Chinese government's claims were rejected by the PCA in a landmark 2016 ruling. The Court concluded that the Chinese "nine dash line" does not grant it historic claims to the resources in those waters. It also ruled that none of the natural features in the Spratly area are "islands" in the legal sense, and therefore none are entitled to a 200 nautical mile exclusive economic zone. At most, some of the features generate a 12 nautical mile territorial sea zone.

It is important to note here that the PCA did not rule on the sovereignty disputes, which is beyond its purview. However, through its findings, the Court clearly raises doubts about China's efforts to exercise both jurisdiction over a presumed EEZ, and

10. Peter Dutton, "Three Disputes and Three Objectives," *Naval War College Review* (Autumn 2011), https://www.usnwc.edu/getattachment/feb516bf-9d93-4d5c-80dc-d5073ad84d9b/Three-Disputes-and-Three-Objectives--China-and-the (accessed February 24, 2017).

11. Chris Chung, "Drawing the U-Shaped Line: China's Claim in the South China Sea, 1946-1974," *Modern China* (January 2016), http://mcx.sagepub.com/content/42/1/38 (accessed February 24, 2017).

12. Hannah Beech, "Just Where Exactly Did China Get the South China Sea Nine-Dash Line From?" *Time* (July 19, 2016), http://time.com/4412191/nine-dash-line-9-south-china-sea/ (accessed February 24, 2017).

control, in which it opposes the freedom of the U.S. Navy to operate.

The Chinese reaction to the PCA ruling has been, at best, intemperate. Having refused to submit to arbitration, Beijing openly derided the findings and questioned the qualifications of the Court and its judges. Chinese Foreign Minister Wang Yi described the ruling as "political farce."[13] China's ambassador to the United States, Cui Tiankai, declared that the tribunal's failure to recognize its lack of jurisdiction was "a matter of professional incompetence," and raised questions of the court's integrity.[14]

China's Coast Guard Supports Chinese Efforts to Dominate the South China Sea

To help underscore China's claims to the South China Sea, substantial resources have been devoted to expanding and strengthening the its coast guard.[15] In 2013, four of China's maritime law enforcement agencies were combined into the Chinese Coast Guard (CCG). This has allowed the PRC to better coordinate its maritime law enforcement activities. While most of its fleet of cutters are unarmed, China is introducing larger and more capable vessels. Several of these appear to be modified versions of the Type 054 frigate already in service in the PLAN.[16] China has also commissioned two coast guard cutters that each displace over 10,000 tons, larger than most World War II cruisers.[17]

These ships serve to intimidate not only fishing boats from neighboring states, but also rival coast guards. Being larger and also more heavily armed, China's newest coast guard vessels clearly have the edge in the event of a clash.

As important, they have been actively intervened against various neighbors' vessels. In 2014, CCG vessels were part of the flotilla protecting the Chinese deep sea oil rig HY981 from Vietnamese vessels, as it began operations in disputed waters. In 2016, a CCG vessel reportedly rammed a Chinese fishing boat that had been seized by Indonesian authorities for operating in Indonesian waters. The CCG vessel apparently sought to get the Indonesians to relinquish the boat.[18] This follows an incident in 2013 where a Chinese vessel armed with machine guns had confronted Indonesian authorities who had seized a Chinese fishing boat found fishing in Indonesian waters. "Outgunned and fearing the Chinese ship might open fire, the Indonesian captain complied...."[19] A CSIS report concluded that "of the 46 major incidents identified in the South China Sea between 2010 and 2016, at least one CCG (or other Chinese maritime law enforcement) vessel was involved in 72 percent of incidents."[20]

The use of law enforcement vessels, however, also serves as a political message. It underscores the idea that the disputed territories and waters are, in fact, Chinese. Just as one does not employ military forces to patrol the streets of one's own city, Beijing's use of law enforcement vessels underscores that it is enforcing its laws, i.e., that the waters and territories are under Chinese jurisdiction.

China's Military Modernization Helps Support Its Claims

However, China's activities in the South China Sea are not solely limited to civilian agencies. Indeed, there has been a steadily expanding military

13. "Chinese Foreign Minister Says South Sea Arbitration a Political Farce," Xinhua (July 13, 2016), http://news.xinhuanet.com/english/2016-07/13/c_135508275.htm (accessed February 24, 2017).

14. Chen Weihua, "China Envoy Blasts Hague Ruling," *China Daily*, July 13, 2016, http://usa.chinadaily.com.cn/epaper/2016-07/13/content_26071163.htm (accessed February 24, 2017).

15. U.S. Navy, Office of Naval Intelligence, *The PLA Navy: New Capabilities and Missions for the 21st Century* (2015), 2015_PLA_NAVY_PUB_Print.pdf (accessed February 24, 2017).

16. Andrew Tate, "China Builds More Armed Coast Guard Ships," *Jane's Defence Weekly*, November 3, 2016. http://www.janes.com/article/65089/china-builds-more-armed-coastguard-ships (accessed February 24, 2017).

17. Kyle Mizokami, "China Launches Another Monster Coast Guard Cutter," *Popular Mechanics*, January 14, 2016, http://www.popularmechanics.com/military/navy-ships/a18990/china-launches-second-monster-coast-guard-cutter/ (accessed February 24, 2017).

18. Joe Cochrane, "China's Coast Guard Rams Fishing Boat to Free It from Indonesian Authorities," *The New York Times*, March 21, 2016, https://www.nytimes.com/2016/03/22/world/asia/indonesia-south-china-sea-fishing-boat.html (accessed February 24, 2017).

19. Ibid.

20. Center for Strategic and International Studies, "Are Maritime Law Enforcement Forces Destabilizing Asia?" http://chinapower.csis.org/maritime-forces-destabilizing-asia/ (accessed February 24, 2017).

component in Chinese actions in this region. This latter effort includes the steady deployment of Chinese military power to the artificial islands it has constructed. Both government and think-tank analyses have indicated that China has now constructed revetments and aircraft shelters typically associated with military air bases, military radar facilities, as well as deployed anti-aircraft guns. Just this past week, new construction was identified typically associated with long range surface-to-air missile (SAM) sites, such as the HQ-9, the Chinese counterpart to the Patriot air defense system.[21]

These deployments are in direct contradiction of the commitment made by Xi Jinping to President Barack Obama in September 2015. At that time, the Chinese leader pledged that "relevant construction activities that China are undertaking in the Nansha (Spratly) Islands do not target or impact any country, and China does not intend to pursue militarization."[22]

Chinese activities in the area have not been restricted to just the artificial islands, however. Chinese naval forces have also sought to influence and intimidate other claimants. Chinese navy task forces have repeatedly sailed around James Shoal, for example, with Chinese press reporting that the crews "swore to safeguard its sovereignty."[23]

These deployments draw upon the steady modernization of the PLA Navy (PLAN). Over the past several years, the PLA Navy has introduced several new classes of surface combatants. The newest Chinese destroyer, the Type 052D, is comparable to the American DDG-51 *Arleigh Burke*-class. The Chinese Type 054A frigate is both more capable and more reliable than either American Littoral Combat Ship design, both types now having been repeatedly sidelined due to engineering problems. Meanwhile, the Chinese are producing multiple classes of submarines, and a new aircraft carrier is under construction. China's naval combatants are among the youngest in average age, thanks to this major shipbuilding program underway.

As important, the Chinese are not neglecting the key issue of support. China is also building a fleet-train of logistics support ships. Chinese submarines operating in the Indian Ocean have been accompanied by submarine tenders, allowing them to operate for longer periods away from Chinese ports. China, of course, has recently begun construction on a new facility in Djibouti, their first formal overseas military base, but probably not their last.

Given the importance of airpower for the Asia Pacific region, it is also worth noting how the PLA Air Force, or PLAAF, is working on the J-20 and J-31 fifth-generation fighters, the only other nation to be working on two stealth fighter programs at the same time. Chinese bombers have overflown various islands in the South China Sea. These aircraft can be equipped with long-range anti-ship and land-attack cruise missiles, sending a clear signal to China's neighbors.

As with their navy, the PLAAF is not neglecting the haft of the spear, even as they sharpen the tip. The PLAAF is fielding new transport aircraft that will allow them to project power across the region. And the PLAAF has displayed new electronic warfare aircraft, as well as AWACS-type aircraft, in recent military parades and exercises.

Most worrisome is the new PLA Strategic Support Force (PLASSF), which brings together under one service space warfare, electronic warfare, and network warfare capabilities. This reflects the ongoing Chinese effort at being able to establish "information dominance," which the PLA considers critical to fighting and winning future wars. It is likely that there will be redoubled Chinese activity in these crucial domains, and application of them against local militaries and governments, as the PLASSF establishes itself and determines a new operational tempo.

Military Modernization Supports Extending Chinese Sovereignty

The objective of all these various force improvements, at the military level, is not solely to support China's claims in the South China Sea. Instead, they mark the steady shift of the PLAN's focus from a "near-shore" strategy of the 1960s, through the "near

---

21. Idrees Ali, "Exclusive: China Finishing South China Sea Buildings that Could House Missiles—US Officials," *Reuters*, February 22, 2017, http://www.reuters.com/article/us-china-usa-southchinasea-exclusive-idUSKBN161029 (accessed February 24, 2017).

22. David Brunnstrom and Michael Martina, "Xi Denies China Turning Artificial Islands Into Military Bases," *Reuters*, September 25, 2015, http://www.reuters.com/article/us-usa-china-pacific-idUSKCN0RP1ZH20150925 (accessed February 24, 2017).

23. Erik Slavin, "Chinese Navy Makes Presence Felt at Disputed Shoal," *Stars and Stripes*, March 27, 2013, http://www.stripes.com/news/pacific/chinese-navy-makes-presence-felt-at-disputed-shoal-1.213662, and "Chinese Ships Patrol Area Contested by Malaysia," *Reuters*, January 26, 2014, http://uk.reuters.com/article/uk-china-malaysia-idUKBREA0P06X20140126 (accessed February 24, 2017).

sea" strategy of the 1990s to today's approach of the "far seas." This steady evolution seeks to push Chinese military capability to ever more extended distance from its shores.

This military shift is not only a reflection of China's growing capabilities, however, but reflects a broader transition in Chinese strategic thinking, affecting both the military and the nation as a whole.

For the military, this ever extending reach is part of the PLA's "new historic missions" or the "missions for the new phase of the new century." Never forgetting that the PLA is a Party-army, the armed wing of the Chinese Communist Party, where every officer above second lieutenant is a member of the party, it has been charged with the responsibility of defending both Party and national interests. This has gone beyond keeping the Party in power and maintaining the ability to take Taiwan (still a central, strategic goal) to safeguarding Chinese interests in key new domains, including the seas, outer space, and the electromagnetic spectrum.

In this regard, there is concern that Beijing may either announce an air defense identification zone or ADIZ over the South China Sea, or simply start behaving as though it has one. The reports that China is constructing facilities intended to house long-range SAM systems, coupled with the construction of runways that would support fighter operations, suggest that such a move could occur in the near future. The creation of a South China Sea ADIZ would further increase tension in the region, and likely compel various states to propose their own ADIZs in response.

U.S. Responses to Chinese Actions

The U.S. government, including the U.S. Congress, needs to pay continued attention to developments in the South China Sea. It needs to make clear that Chinese efforts to expand its sovereignty into international common spaces will not continue unimpeded.

One important element needs to be a clear enunciation of the position that the United States considers the PCA's findings as the basis for international law. It is essential to counter China's efforts at legal warfare and psychological warfare in the region by making clear that China's positions have no legal standing. By remaining quiet on this issue, Washington cedes the political high ground.

Another essential aspect is to explore non-military means of degrading China's efforts at artificial island construction. The focus should be on discouraging and frustrating the activities of the companies

that participate in China's land reclamation efforts in the South China Sea. If the United States were to deny Chinese companies involved in Chinese artificial island building access to the American market, that could well prove a substantial deterrent to working on such projects. This would be even more true if the U.S. could persuade other states to impose comparable restrictions. One Chinese company, CCCC Dredging, for example, is reportedly extensively involved in Chinese land reclamation efforts; it is apparently also intent on establishing a worldwide presence in the dredging business. A concerted effort by the U.S., Japan, and European countries, as well as others, to deny the company access to their markets would compel CCCC Dredging to choose between South China Sea activities and its global ambitions.

Similarly, the dozens of dredgers that have been photographed in the Spratlys area are all complex pieces of equipment, involving equipment such as trailing suction hopper dredgers and the like. Some of these systems are imported, while others use parts and sub-systems that are supplied from a variety of commercial vendors, rather than specially fabricated by the People's Liberation Army (PLA). If the United States and key allies in places like Europe and Japan were to act to prevent third party companies from supporting Chinese reclamation efforts in the South China Sea, it would certainly affect Chinese ability to sustain such activities in the future.

This would not prevent the PRC from manufacturing its own dredging equipment, but, again, the market for such items may be limited if the United States were to spearhead a global effort to deny Chinese companies partners and market presence in Europe, Japan, North America, and Australia, or their use by Western companies in contracts abroad (e.g., the Middle East, South America).

Another means of influencing Chinese companies may be to deny them the ability to list on the American stock exchanges. Listing there is not only a means of raising capital, but is also often seen as a stamp of approval, since it requires complying with American rules about financial stability and transparency. Limiting access to American (and Western) capital markets and denying them legitimacy could prove an effective instrument.

Additionally, the U.S. could, in the coming years, help expand deep sea exploration by other claimants to the South China Sea region. China has been striving to exclude all other states from engaging in oil exploration in this area, even as Beijing pursues it. The incidents involving Chinese oil rig HY981 in 2014 saw China deploy its deep sea oil rig to disputed waters off Vietnam. This move was supported by statements by senior Chinese officials that oil rigs are "mobile national territory." American efforts to help local states develop their own "mobile national territory" could serve as a means of challenging China's excessive claims—and not only in the South China Sea.

Backing such economic moves must be the United States Coast Guard and Navy. In particular, the U.S. should study the requirements for deploying U.S. Coast Guard cutters and other vessels to the South China Sea as part of the broader array of Freedom of Navigation Operations (FONOPS). By deploying its own "white hulls," the U.S. could avoid accusations that it is escalating tensions in the South China Sea, while nonetheless signaling its rejection of China's expansive claims. U.S. Coast Guard vessels already operate overseas, and have even at times had to threaten the use of force in the course of their duties.[24] The U.S. should propose joint patrols in disputed areas, to make clear that it is intent upon preserving freedom of the seas—and is not taking a position on sovereignty. At the same time, by expanding cooperation with other regional coast guards, Washington would be making clear that its commitment to the region is not solely a military one.

***

The Heritage Foundation is a public policy, research, and educational organization recognized as exempt under section 501(c)(3) of the Internal Revenue Code. It is privately supported and receives no funds from any government at any level, nor does it perform any government or other contract work.

The Heritage Foundation is the most broadly supported think tank in the United States. During 2016, it had hundreds of thousands of individual, foundation, and corporate supporters representing every state in the U.S. Its 2016 income came from the following sources:

Individuals 75.3%

Foundations 20.3%

Corporations 1.8%

Program revenue and other income 2.6%

The top five corporate givers provided The Heritage Foundation with 1.0% of its 2016 income. The Heritage Foundation's books are audited annually by the national accounting firm of RSM US, LLP.

24. Hendrick Simoes, "Coast Guard Team Fires Shot at Iranian Dhow in Persian Gulf," *Stars and Stripes*, August 27, 2014, http://www.stripes.com/news/middle-east/coast-guard-team-fires-shot-at-iranian-dhow-in-persian-gulf-1.300099 (accessed February 24, 2017).

Mr. YOHO. Thank you, and I appreciate your testimony. And those are the things we want to gain out of this. You know, we will come back to some of your comments that I have questions on.

Dr. Auslin, if you would go ahead.

STATEMENT OF MICHAEL AUSLIN, PH.D., RESIDENT SCHOLAR, DIRECTOR OF JAPAN STUDIES, AMERICAN ENTERPRISE INSTITUTE

Mr. AUSLIN. Mr. Chairman, Ranking Member Sherman, members of the committee, I am honored to speak before you today on the issue of U.S. maritime strategy in Asia. With a new administration, it is a particularly timely moment to do so. I believe it is also time to adopt a larger geostrategic picture of the entire Asia-Pacific region. Seeing the South China Sea, the East China Sea, and the Yellow Sea as one integrated strategic space or what we might refer to as the Asiatic Mediterranean.

The United States maintains several enduring interests in maritime East Asia. First, since the close of World War II, we have sought to prevent the emergence of a hostile hegemon that could dominate our partners or eventually threaten the U.S. mainland. U.S. forward-based military forces along Asia's first island chain have served to deter full-scale war in Asia for more than six decades.

Second, the U.S. maintains an interest in preserving our network of allies and partners in the region. American alliances remain a fundamental source of our strength in the world.

Third, the U.S. retains an interest in defending the free flow of trade and commerce through Asia's waterways. Annually, $5.3 trillion of trade passes through the South China Sea. U.S. trade accounts for $1.2 trillion of this total.

There are numerous threats to U.S. interests or potential threats to U.S. interests that may emerge in the future. From a domestic political perspective, Beijing views its maritime claims in the South and East China Seas as what it calls "blue national soil." Foreign claims to the Spratly and Paracel Islands are an infringement, in Beijing's view, on its sovereign territory, and Chinese leaders have hardened their public positions on the South China Sea over time. China's nine-dash line encompasses 90 percent of the South China Sea. While Beijing remains vague about its claims to the waters and airspace within the line, it considers the area to be historically Chinese waters. To both defend its maritime claims and protect its southeastern flank, Beijing has spent the past three decades building its military power projection capabilities out to dispersed island chain and beyond, developing anti-access/area denial technology and naval forces to challenge the U.S. military in its near seas.

Over the past two decades, Chinese ships have harassed, shadowed, and interfered with the activities of U.S. naval assets operating in its near seas. While in the East China Sea, the PRC continues to challenge Japan's administration of the Senkakus by frequently sailing flotillas of fishing boats, coast guard ships, and maritime militias in and around the Senkakus territorial waters. By slowly changing the situation on the ground or on the water, China hopes to transform the Asiatic Mediterranean into a Chinese lake. Chinese control of the South China Sea at the exclusion of the U.S. is obviously not a fait accompli, but we must act to implement a counter coercion strategy if we hope to maintain assured access to Asia's littorals.

Let me mention a few policy recommendations. First, we should demonstrate diplomatic leadership. Washington's network of allies and partners throughout the Asia Pacific remains the backbone of our engagement in the region. The first order of business for the Trump administration is to continue energetic diplomacy throughout the region, to assure allied capitals, and signal to the China that we remain committed.

Later this year, I hope to see the administration send high-level attendees to the June Shangri-La dialogue, the August ASEAN regional forum, and the November East Asia and APEC summits. Diplomatic jaw-jaw alone, however, is insufficient. We must also strengthen economic ties with our liberal allies in the region. While the current administration has declared the Trans-Pacific Partnership dead, it has remained open to the possibility of bilateral free-trade agreements. If it pursues this path, then the best place for President Trump to start would be with Japan.

In addition, we must engage in more multilateral security cooperation. It is incumbent on the U.S. to attempt to better train and equip the forces of Southeast Asian nations as well as our allies and partners to resist coercion and intimidation by the Chinese Navy and raise the cost of Beijing's salami-slicing strategy in the East Asia Seas.

I believe the U.S. must continue to raise foreign military financing levels in Southeast Asia. In 2015, Congress authorized a $28 million East Asia-Pacific foreign military financing fund that could be disbursed to various Southeast Asian nations as needed. This pot of money should be renewed annually. The U.S. should also encourage regional players to engage in these cooperative security efforts including our allies in Japan, Australia, and South Korea.

And, finally, we should reinforce these efforts with U.S. hard power. We should increase the tempo of our Freedom of Navigation operations in the region, not as a provocation but as a signal that we will defend our rights in accordance with international law.

We must be more willing to use coercive diplomacy to raise the costs on China and against its actions against our allies or our interests.

The goal, in conclusion, is not to back the Chinese into a corner or goad them into further aggression but, rather, just the opposite. They must understand that unprovoked and belligerent acts will merit a rejoinder; otherwise, they will get the wrong message and continue testing the U.S. Government and our allies.

Thank you.

[The prepared statement of Mr. Auslin follows:]

Statement before the House Committee on Foreign Affairs
Subcommittee on Asia and the Pacific
on 'Checking China's Maritime Push'

Securing 'Asia's Mediterranean'

Michael R. Auslin
Resident Scholar and Director of Japan Studies

February 28, 2017

Mr. Chairman and members of the committee, I'm honored to speak before you today on the issue of US maritime strategy in East Asia.

In Washington foreign policy circles, we tend to compartmentalize Asia's maritime domain into separate spaces by speaking as if what happens in the South China Sea doesn't impact events in the East China Sea, and so on. I believe that this approach is fundamentally incorrect. By attempting to segregate Asia's littorals, we hinder our ability to see the growing threats to US national security interests across maritime East Asia as a whole.

Instead, it is time to adopt a larger geostrategic picture of the entire Asia-Pacific region. To do so, we must see the South China Sea, East China Sea, and Yellow Sea as one integrated strategic space, or what I refer to as the "Asiatic Mediterranean."[1] The geopolitical challenge the United States and its allies and partners face is an emerging struggle for control for the entire common maritime space of eastern Asia.

US Interests in Maritime East Asia

The United States maintains several enduring interests in maritime East Asia.

First, since the close of World War II, the United States has sought to maintain a preponderance of power on both ends of the Eurasian landmass by seeking to prevent the emergence of a hostile hegemon that could threaten the US mainland. US forward-based military forces along Asia's "first island chain" have served to deter full-scale war in Asia for more than six decades, allowing Asia to develop into the prosperous and free region we see today.

The People's Republic of China (PRC) is a rising power with hegemonic ambitions in the Asia-Pacific region. While the Sino-American relationship contains a mixture of cooperative and competitive dynamics, Washington must be prepared to compete with Beijing as it seeks to reduce US influence in the region.

A struggle for control of the "inner seas" (such as the South and East China Seas) is often the first step to a larger contest over controlling the periphery of the Eurasian landmass. For historical examples of this phenomenon, look to the decades-long war waged by the British Royal Navy against Napoleon's ships in the English Channel and French littoral waters, as well as the Imperial Japanese Navy's reduction of the Chinese and Russian fleets in the Yellow Sea in both 1894 and 1904, giving it control of access to Korea and China. Today, we are engaged in a struggle with Beijing to maintain control over Asia's inner seas.

Second, the US maintains an interest in preserving our network of allies and partners in the region. American alliances remain a fundamental source of our strength in the world. The Trump administration is right to revisit conversations about fair and proper burden-sharing in US alliances, however, I worry that many Americans take the existence of these alliances for granted.

Japan and Germany, the third- and fourth-largest economies in the world, are both examples of former adversaries that are now among Washington's closest security allies and trading partners. Additionally, as late as 1987, South Korea was a backward authoritarian state, which has now transformed into a thriving democracy and a steadfast US ally. South Korea imports more than $40 billion in American goods annually that support nearly 200,000 American jobs.[2] US economic and security interests are well served by our enduring alliances in the Asia-Pacific.

The US is a treaty ally with five nations in the Asia-Pacific. Additionally, we continue to develop stronger partnerships with countries including Singapore, Vietnam, and Taiwan. All these states are threatened by China's expansive maritime and territorial claims. A Chinese conflict with the Philippines over Scarborough Shoal or with the Japanese over the Senkaku Islands would surely draw in the United States.

Third, the US retains an interest in defending the free flow of trade and commerce through Asia's waterways. Annually, $5.3 trillion of trade passes through the South China Sea—US trade accounts for $1.2 trillion of this total.[3] More than 30 percent of the world's liquefied natural gas passes through the Straits of Malacca and into the South China Sea.[4] Nearly 60 percent of Japan, South Korea, and Taiwan's energy supplies, as well as 80 percent of China's crude oil imports, flow through the South China Sea.[5] In short, the health of the global economy depends on freedom of navigation through these waterways.

Imagine the damage to US markets and US consumers if cargo ships bound for ports in Los Angeles, Oakland, and Seattle were stopped transiting the South China Sea. While not likely in the immediate future, it is time for US strategists and policymakers to understand the attendant risks of allowing a competitor (in this case the PRC) to dominate crucial waterways in Asia.

Threats to US Interests

US media outlets have well-documented China's militarization of its near seas over the past two years, but I'll attempt to explain how China's island building fits into a larger strategy to dominate its maritime periphery.

From a domestic political perspective, Beijing views its maritime claims in the South and East China Seas as "blue national soil."[6] Foreign claims to the Spratly and Parcel Islands are infringement on its sovereign territory. Chinese leaders have hardened their public positions on the South China over time. Former premier Wen Jiabao stated that the South China Sea has been "China's historical territory since ancient times."[7] The Chinese Communist Party's legitimacy is tied to its promise to restore China to its former position of greatness or centrality in Asia. Any effort to bargain or negotiate over its "blue territory" would be viewed by the Chinese public as ceding sovereignty to foreign powers.

China's nine-dash line encompasses 90 percent of the South China Sea. While Beijing remains vague about its claims to the waters and airspace within the line, it considers the area to be historically Chinese waters. China has declared straight baselines around the Paracel Island group to demarcate its territorial waters—a clear violation of UNCLOS. China also has declared military alert zones around its artificial Spratly Island features.

To enter the mind of a Chinese defense strategist, I find it useful to examine an upside down map of China's maritime coast line. Hemming in China's coastline is the "first island chain"—a ring of islands running northeast from the Indian Ocean up to the Kamchatka Peninsula. Along that chain, a Chinese defense planner would see US forces based in South Korea, Japan, and the Philippines. In addition, the US maintains its military support for Taiwan, the "unsinkable aircraft carrier" sitting just off of China's coast.[8] It is entirely understandable for China to feel insecure with its maritime flank exposed to foreign powers.

To both defend its maritime claims and protect its southeastern flank, Beijing has spent the past three decades building its military power projection capabilities out to this first island chain and beyond, developing anti-access area-denial (A2/AD) technology and naval forces to challenge the US military in its near seas.

Beijing has used what analysts typically call a "salami slicing" strategy to exert control over its near seas. By slowly changing facts on the ground via incremental steps, the Chinese have stayed below the threshold of a forceful US response. For example, to date China has constructed 3,000 acres of artificial "islands" in the Spratly and Paracel island chains. China's biggest South China Sea bases, at Fiery Cross, Subi, and Mischief Reef, all have "10,000 foot runways, deep water harbors, and enough reinforced hangars to house 24 fighters as well as bombers, tankers, and airborne early warning aircraft."[9] For comparisons sake, Mischief Reef's "land perimeter is nearly the size of the perimeter of the District of Columbia."[10] Subi Reef's deep-water harbor is more than two miles wide—or as large as Pearl Harbor's. The point being that these bases are not "sand castles" in the sea, but rather formidable centers of power projection.

While developing island infrastructure, the Chinese have enveloped contested areas of the South China Sea with coast guard and fishing fleets to enforce its claims. These irregular forces constantly "probe" US and smaller, regional states to see how far it can push before it receives a response.

Over the past two decades, Chinese ships have harassed, shadowed, and interfered with the activities of US naval assets operating in its near seas.[11] Recently, US surveillance planes in the South China Sea have received multiple warnings from the Chinese navy as they approached so-called "military alert zones" around Chinese occupied islands.[12] There are also reports that Chinese forces have attempted to jam US surveillance drones conducting missions over the South China Sea.[13]

Recently, China has used the guise of "maritime traffic safety" to harass US assets. In December 2016, Chinese forces seized an unmanned, underwater US Navy drone in international waters off the Philippine coast, claiming that it did so "to prevent it from harming navigational and personnel safety of passing ships."[14] Now, reports indicate that Beijing is considering a maritime traffic safety law that would require foreign submarines to stay surfaced and display their national flag while in Chinese waters.[15] It's unclear what Beijing means by Chinese waters. I certainly anticipate the US navy will not cooperate.

In the East China Sea, the PRC continues to challenge Japan's administration of the Senkaku Islands by frequently sailing flotillas of fishing boats, coast guard ships, and maritime militias in and around the Senkakus' territorial waters. For example, in August 2016, 300 Chinese fishing boats arrived under the escort of 28 coast guard ships to challenge the Japanese.[16] Meanwhile, in the airspace above the East China Sea, PLA Air Force jets and bombers regularly fly near Japanese airspace to test the Japanese Self-Defense Force (JSDF). Between April and September of 2016, the JSDF conducted more than 400 intercepts of Chinese military aircraft encroaching on its airspace.[17] I fully expect the Chinese to maintain or increase these high-tempo maritime and aerial probes against Tokyo.

By slowly changing the situation on the ground, China hopes to transform "Asia Mediterranean" into a Chinese lake. Chinese control of the South China Sea at the exclusion of the US is not yet a fait accompli, but the US must act urgently to implement a counter-coercion strategy if we hope to maintain assured access to Asia's littorals.

Policy Recommendations

Demonstrate Diplomatic Leadership. Washington's network of allies and partners throughout the Asia-Pacific remain the backbone of our engagement in the region. The first order of business for the Trump administration is to continue energetic diplomacy throughout the region to assure allied capitals and signal to the Chinese that we remain committed to the region.

While I have criticized the Obama administration's lack of execution of its so-called "pivot" to Asia, I do give the past administration's Asia-policy team a great deal of credit for energizing US diplomatic engagement in the region. In her first four years as secretary of state, Hillary Clinton made 62 visits to Asian countries.[18] The Obama administration signed ASEAN Treaty of Amity and Cooperation in 2009 and invested substantive diplomatic capital in the East Asia Summit as well.

Thus far, the Trump administration is off to a strong start with the February 2017 Trump-Abe summit in Mar-a-Lago Florida, as well as Secretary of Defense James Mattis' recent visit to both Tokyo and Seoul. US officials continue to reassure Tokyo that the Senkaku Islands fall under Article 5 of the mutual defense treaty. President Trump, Secretary Rex Tillerson, and Secretary Mattis have all assured their Japanese counterparts of this fact on separate occasions over the past month.

Later this year, I hope to see the administration send high-level attendees to the June Shangri-La Dialogue, August ASEAN Regional Forum, and November East Asia and APEC Summits. Cabinet-level attendance at these summits is vital as the US pushes back on China's false narrative that the US is militarizing maritime East Asia. At all of these summits, US leaders should continue to highlight the 2016 Hague Arbitral Tribunal ruling that invalidated China's nine-dash line claim to the South China Sea and declared that none of the features in the Spratly islands are legally islands entitled to expansive maritime entitlements.

Diplomatic "jaw-jaw" alone, however, is not sufficient. The US must also take concrete steps to strengthen our partnerships. One way to do so is by strengthening economic ties with our liberal allies in the region. While the current administration had declared the Trans-Pacific Partnership (TPP) dead, it has remained open to the possibility of bilateral free trade agreements.

The best place for President Trump to start would be with Japan. Total trade in goods and services between the two countries reached $283 billion in 2014. Although the trade in goods has been flat, if not in slight decline for more than two decades, services have increased. Even with agricultural restrictions, Japan remains a major market for US farmers. Between 1998 and 2011, US investment in Japan doubled. According to the East-West Center, every US state exports at least $100 million in goods and services to Japan every year, while fully 31 states export $1 billion or more. (California, not surprisingly, exports the most at $20 billion.)

For its part, Japan is the second-largest foreign investor in the United States, after the United Kingdom, with $373 billion in US holdings. Its main exports include machinery, electronics, and optical and medical instruments. The Japanese automobile industry, which began shifting production to the United States in the 1980s, employs 1.36 million American workers directly or indirectly, according to trade association figures. Just as importantly, numerous small and midsize Japanese firms are integral parts of the high-tech global supply chain for consumer items such smart phones, smart televisions, and the like.

The framework for a US-Japanese bilateral free trade agreement (FTA) already exists in the TPP. Indeed, hints from the Trump team that they want to renegotiate, not simply trash current trade agreements, means the two sides could jump start bilateral negotiations by basing them on modified parts of the TPP. Whether that will satisfy Trump's demands for transparency and simplicity is unknown, but elements of the TPP not relevant to the trade between two advanced countries, such as on state-owned enterprises, easily can be dropped. Similarly, given the high labor and environmental standards in both countries, other relevant chapters may be simplified.

Still, a US-Japanese bilateral FTA needs to include the agreements made on scrapping long-standing restrictions on US products in Japan. Thus, the TPP chapters related to reducing nontariff barriers on autos and eliminating tariffs on American dairy products, wine, beef and pork, and soybeans should be replicated. Since Japan is America's largest overseas beef market, accounting for $1.6 billion in sales, even with a 38.5 percent tariff, as well as being a major importer of US pork and soybeans (even with 21 percent tariff), ensuring a level playing field should be the top priority for the Trump administration in any bilateral negotiations.

Negotiating a bilateral free-trade pact would further strengthen the strategic basis of US-Japanese relations. Next the US could consider a similar pact with Taiwan.

Engage in Multilateral Security Cooperation. While Japan maintains a well-trained and equipped force, the coast guards and navies of US Southeast Asia partners are badly outmatched by the Chinese. China's coast guard today is larger than the combined naval forces of Japan, Indonesia, Vietnam, the Philippines, and Malaysia.[19] For example, in April 2012, China seized the Scarborough Shoal from Manila, a feature only 100 nautical miles off the Philippine coast. Then in May 2014, China moved an oil rig 120 miles off the coast of Vietnam causing a standoff with Hanoi.

The US navy does not have the capacity or responsibility to respond to every act of Chinese coercion against our partners. However, the collective result of these Chinese actions is a changing balance of power in the South China Sea. Therefore, it is incumbent on the US to better train and equip these forces to resist the PRC and raise the costs of Beijing's "salami slicing" strategy.

Currently, the US only devotes around 1 percent of its foreign military financing (FMF) budget to the Asia-Pacific region.[20] Recognizing the shortfall in Title 22 security assistance to the region, the Obama administration, in partnership with SASC Chairman John McCain turned to Title 10 authorities, launching the Southeast Asia Maritime Security Initiative (MSI) last year to improve regional maritime domain awareness for Indonesia, Malaysia, the Philippines, Thailand, and Vietnam. The program will provide $425 million to these nations over five years.

While the MSI program is a positive step in aiding US partners in the region, I believe the US must continue to also raise FMF levels in Southeast Asia. Starting in 2015, Congress authorized a $28 million East Asia-Pacific FMF fund that could be disbursed to various Southeast Asian states as needed.[21] I believe it's important for Congress to continue to renew this pot of money annually.

The United States should also encourage regional players to engage in these cooperative security efforts. US allies, such as Japan, Australia, and South Korea, have maritime interests and can provide coast guard and C4ISR assets to Southeast Asian states facing Chinese coercion. These allies are a vital force multiplier for US efforts in the region.

Tokyo has already become more active in the region, over concern for China's ability to cut off the maritime trade routes that serve as Japan's economic lifeline. Under Prime Minister Abe's "proactive contribution to peace" policy, Tokyo has signed strategic partnership agreements with Indonesia, Malaysia, the Philippines, and Vietnam. Japan has agreed to provide patrol ships and aircraft to these nations as well. As US-Philippine ties have soured under President Duterte's administration, Tokyo has continued to provide new security assistance packages to Manilla. Despite the past few months of rocky relations, the US still maintains a long-term interest in building the Philippines' defense capacity. The networked nature of our alliance with Japan will allow this progress to continue.

In the short term, Southeast Asia states badly need maritime domain awareness capabilities including radars, patrol planes, coast guard cutters, and drones. However, over the medium term, the US should work with Southeast Asian partner states to develop their own A2/AD capabilities to deter Chinese aggression. This would involve the acquisition of antiship cruise missiles, mobile antiaircraft systems, smart sea mines, and antisubmarine warfare systems. By developing their own asymmetric strategies, US partners will be better prepared to complicate Chinese defense planning.

Reinforce These Efforts with US Hard Power. From 2012 to 2015, as the Chinese were in the midst of their island building spree in the South China Sea, the Obama administration did not publicly approve FONOPS near or around China's outposts in the South China Sea. After facing sustained public pressure, the Obama administration approved four FONOPS in 2015–16. The administration chose to use these missions as a highly public signal of resolve to the Chinese. But the damage already had been done. Today, each time the US sails a naval flotilla into the South China Sea, its considered front page news by CNN. This should not be the case, as the US Navy has been conducting FONOPs in these seas for decades. We need to reestablish FONOPs as business as usual.

I believe the US needs to increase the tempo of its FONOPs missions in the region, not as a provocation of the Chinese, but rather as a signal that we will defend our rights in accordance with international law. Several experts have proposed that the next US FONOP should challenge China's claim to Mischief Reef in the Spratly Islands.[22] The Hague tribunal ruled that Mischief was a low-tide elevation that is not entitled to a territorial sea, exclusive economic zone, or continental shelf. With that said, I leave the tactical deliberations to the Office of the Secretary of Defense and the US Navy.

The Chinese will continue to challenge and harass US naval vessels operating in the South China Sea. The US navy will be asked to operate in contested strategic space, something we have not had to do since the Cold War. A robust FONOP package may require occasionally rubbing paint with Chinese coast guard or PLAN ships. This approach inherently requires our policymakers to tolerate higher levels of risk. The fundamental question facing our leadership is whether they can tolerate that risk. For two decades the US has enjoyed a "unipolar moment" free from great power competition. But now regional powers have begun to probe and challenge the front lines of American power. Are we willing to compete at sea?

In addition to a robust FONOP program, I believe that the US must be more willing to use coercive diplomacy to raise the costs of further Chinese belligerence against US or allied maritime forces in East Asia. This policy menu should include reducing military contacts and disinviting the Chinese navy from RIMPAC naval exercises, considering targeted sanctions against Chinese companies connected to the military, and refusing visas for high-ranking Chinese officials.

The goal is not to back the Chinese into a corner or goad them into further aggression, but rather just the opposite. Beijing must understand that such unprovoked and belligerent acts will merit a rejoinder. Otherwise, China will get the wrong message and will continue testing the US government.

Conclusion

The US cannot rollback China's artificial islands in the South China Sea, however, we can pressure China's maritime strategy throughout "Asia's Mediterranean." Using energetic diplomacy, we can continue to signal to Beijing, while also assuring our allies and partners, that Washington will continue to "fly, sail, and operate wherever international law allows," to borrow a line from former Secretary of Defense Ash Carter.[33] By working with our wealthy Asian allies, we should continue to provide badly needed defense capabilities to our Southeast Asian partners. Beijing should no longer be able to encroach on the maritime rights of US partner nations uncontested.

Most importantly, the US must elevate its own tolerance for risk in maritime East Asia. By conducting FONOPs in and around China's illegal claims, we will bring our forces into close proximity with Chinese assets. In threatening sanctions or reduced military contact with the Chinese, we should expect pushback and even retaliation from Beijing. But these are steps we must be prepared to take if we hope to deter Beijing from continued maritime expansion.

Washington must accept the reality of China's revisionism. If we do not, I fear that in the near future, the US will be unable to retain assured access to the vital waterways of East Asia.

Notes

[1] Michael Auslin, "Asia's Mediterranean: Strategy, Geopolitics, and Risk in the Sea of the Indo-Pacific," *War on the Rocks*, February 29, 2016, https://warontherocks.com/2016/02/asias-mediterranean-strategy-geopolitics-and-risk-in-the-seas-of-the-indo-pacific/.

[2] US Census Bureau, "Trade in Goods with Korea, South," https://www.census.gov/foreign-trade/balance/c5800.html; and "Remarks by the President at the Announcement of a U.S.-Korea Free Trade Agreement," White House, December 4, 2017, https://obamawhitehouse.archives.gov/the-press-office/2010/12/04/remarks-president-announcement-a-us-korea-free-trade-agreement.

[3] Bonnie S. Glaser, "Armed Clash in the South China Sea: Contingency Planning Memorandum No. 14," Council on Foreign Relations, April 2015, http://www.cfr.org/asia-and-pacific/armed-clash-south-china-sea/p27883.

[4] Center for Strategic and International Studies, "18 Maps That Explain Maritime Security in Asia," 2014, https://amti.csis.org/atlas/.

[5] Robert D. Kaplan, "The South China Sea Will Be the Battleground of the Future," Business Insider, February 6, 2016, http://www.businessinsider.com/why-the-south-china-sea-is-so-crucial-2015-2.

[6] Office of Naval Intelligence, "The PLA Navy: New Capabilities and Missions for the 21st Century," December 2015, http://www.oni.navy.mil/Portals/12/Intel%20agencies/China_Media/2015_PLA_NAVY_PUB_Print_Low_Res.pdf?ver=2015-12-02-081233-733.

[7] Mohan Malik, "Historical Fiction: China's South China Sea Claims," World Affairs, May/June 2013, http://www.worldaffairsjournal.org/article/historical-fiction-china%E2%80%99s-south-china-sea-claims.

[8] A quote attributed to General Douglas MacArthur.

[9] Thomas Shugart, "China's Artificial Islands Are Bigger (And a Bigger Deal) Than You Think," *War on the Rocks*, September 21, 2016, https://warontherocks.com/2016/09/chinas-artificial-islands-are-bigger-and-a-bigger-deal-than-you-think/.

[10] Ibid.

[11] Including: USNS Bowditch (March 2001), EP-3 Incident (April 2001), USNS Impeccable (March 2009), USS George Washington (July–November 2010), U-2 Intercept (June 2011), USNS Impeccable (July 2013), and UUV seizure (December 2016).

[12] Jim Sciutto, "Exclusive: China Warns U.S. Surveillance Plane," *CNN*, September 15, 2015, http://www.cnn.com/2015/05/20/politics/south-china-sea-navy-flight/.

[13] Bill Gertz, "Chinese Military Using Jamming Against U.S. Drones," *Free Beacon*, May 22, 2015, http://freebeacon.com/national-security/chinese-military-using-jamming-against-u-s-drones/.

[14] Katie Hunt and Steven Jiang, "China: Seized Underwater Drone 'Tip of Iceberg' When It Comes to US Surveillance," *CNN*, December 18, 2016, http://www.cnn.com/2016/12/18/politics/china-us-underwater-vehicle-south-china-sea/.

[15] Steve Mollman, "Now China Wants All Subs in the South China Sea to Ask Permission, Surface, Show Flag," *Defense One*, February 21, 2017, http://www.defenseone.com/threats/2017/02/beijing-wants-limit-foreign-submarine-operations-near-its-south-china-sea-islands/135582/?oref=d-river.

[16] Reiji Yoshida, "Japan Coast Guard releases video showing Chinese intrusions into waters near Senkakus," *Japan Times*, August 16, 2016, http://www.japantimes.co.jp/news/2016/08/16/national/politics-diplomacy/japan-coast-guard-releases-video-showing-chinese-intrusions-waters-near-senkakus/#.WLBdCFUrKpp.

[17] Brad Lendon, "China: Japanese military jets using 'dangerous' tactics," *CNN*, October 28, 2016, http://www.cnn.com/2016/10/27/asia/china-japan-fighter-jet-intercepts/.

[18] Catherine Putz and Shannon Tiezzi, "Did Hillary Clinton's Pivot to Asia Work?" *The Diplomat*, April 15, 2016, http://thediplomat.com/2016/04/did-hillary-clintons-pivot-to-asia-work/.

[19] Office of Naval Intelligence, "The PLA Navy: New Capabilities and Missions for the 21st Century."

[20] Mira Rapp-Hooper et al., "Networked Transparency: Constructing a Common Operational Picture of the South China Sea," Center for a New American Security, March 21, 2016, https://www.cnas.org/publications/reports/networked-transparency-constructing-a-common-operational-picture-of-the-south-china-sea#fn2.

[21] State Department, "Congressional Budget Justification, Foreign Operations Appendix 3, Fiscal Year 2017," https://www.state.gov/documents/organization/252734.pdf.

[22] Bonnie Glaser, Peter Dutton, and Zack Cooper, "Mischief Reef: President Trump's First FONOP?," Center for Strategic and International Studies, Asia Maritime Transparency Initiative, https://amti.csis.org/mischief-reef-president-trump/.

[23] Department of Defense, "Remarks by Secretary Carter and Q&A at the Shangri-La Dialogue, Singapore," June 5, 2016, https://www.defense.gov/News/Transcripts/Transcript-View/Article/791472/remarks-by-secretary-carter-and-qa-at-the-shangri-la-dialogue-singapore.

Mr. YOHO. Thank you for your statement.

And, Dr. Swaine, look forward to hearing yours.

STATEMENT OF MICHAEL D. SWAINE, PH.D., SENIOR FELLOW, ASIA PROGRAM, CARNEGIE ENDOWMENT FOR INTERNATIONAL PEACE

Mr. SWAINE. Thank you very much, Mr. Chairman, members. It is a pleasure to be here today.

Let me speak, first, about the situation in the maritime areas, as I see it. Since roughly 2007, 2008, China has clearly taken a more assertive and active stance toward its longstanding territorial claims in the South and East China Seas, both bordering its long maritime coast. In truth, the historical dynamic at work in the disputed maritime areas has long involved an interactive tit-for-tat rivalry among the claimants made possible by the absence of any clear and commonly accepted code of conduct and driven by deep-seated suspicions and strongly felt nationalist impulses on all sides.

In recent years, however, Beijing has certainly gone beyond such proportional tit-for-tat interaction to apparent attempts to establish itself as the dominant claimant in the Spratly Islands, which are the southern islands in the South China Sea, arguably to deter perceived provocations by others and to establish a strong position in future negotiations, correcting what had been a very weak position in that area.

In the case of the East China Sea dispute with Japan, Beijing has also departed from its past tit-for-tat stance in an attempt to establish itself in recent years as an equal claimant to Tokyo over disputed islands, thereby supposedly correcting years of what it regards as Japanese dominance.

While not taking any formal position in support of any claimant's sovereignty, Washington has clearly focused the vast majority of its concern and its actions since roughly 2010 on Beijing while backing its allies. The obvious danger presented by this situation is that increasing numbers of U.S. allies and Chinese air and naval assets operating in close proximity to one another or perceived provocations of various sorts, including further military deployments onto land features, could produce escalating crises and conflict.

This danger is reinforced by the failure of China, and to a lesser extent other disputants, to clarify their claim regarding various waters. Contrary to widespread claims in the media and elsewhere, Beijing has yet to define exactly what the so-called South China Sea nine-dash line denotes regarding the waters within it. The resulting uncertainty stimulates worst-casing about motives and behavior, thus leading to further escalation.

So what is to be done in this situation? First, I think there needs to be a recognition that a continuous, unilateral U.S. military escalation in presence and activities in an effort to retain a clearcut level of military predominance over China will have, at best, a limited short-term dampening effect on the worsening security competition and would more likely make the situation much worse.

The forces of nationalism, the public visibility of actions taken, the close proximity of the disputed areas to mainland China and Beijing's continued economic and military growth and distrust of

U.S. make a confrontation more, not less, likely under such circumstances.

Moreover, barring an unlikely near total collapse of the Chinese economy and/or a major surge in the overall U.S. GDP, Washington will not possess the capacity to greatly exceed the kind of military and economic capabilities that China will be able to bring to bear in its nearby maritime areas over the coming years.

We are looking at the emergence of a de facto unstable balance of power in the Western Pacific under present conditions.

Second, in place of an open-ended escalation, a stable, enduring modus vivendi among all relevant parties is needed. This should center on agreements to exercise mutual restraint in asserting local sovereign or special rights as well as an effective peaceful process for handling incidents. Such an understanding ideally should consist of several elements. The first is a far greater emphasis on diplomacy than we have seen thus far to establish an interim set of understandings among the claimants and between Beijing and Washington regarding levels and types of militarization and non-use of force. The United States and China must take the lead in this effort based on a common recognition of the need to remove the maritime issue as a driver of their deepening strategic competition.

A second element should include a staged diplomatic process for clarifying the jurisdictional disputes involving both sovereignty issues and nonsovereignty rights over resource extraction such as fishing. Washington must do more to facilitate this effort and not leave it simply to Beijing and the other disputants to determine. During this process, Beijing would need to clarify the meaning of the nine-dash line, and all claimants would specify their claim to land or underwater features and corresponding waters as well as so-called historical rights ideally as they relate to relevant legal definitions under UNCLOS.

Third, on the basis of such clarification of claims and jurisdictions, all parties in the South China Sea and East China Sea disputes must reach an agreement on those areas subject to joint resource development and a procedure for implementing such development.

Finally, on the basis of the previous actions, the claimants must eventually negotiate elements of a binding code of conduct for limiting levels of militarization and handling future incidents over the long term. Obviously, many obstacles would confront any efforts to greatly reduce disputes over maritime territory claims. And American leverage is extremely limited in this area because of its failure to ratify UNCLOS. How can Washington seriously press China and others to abide by UNCLOS rulings and establish a code of conduct when it refuses to subject itself to such scrutiny? These obstacles are not insurmountable however, especially if they are placed within a larger effort to create an overall regional balance of power, and they must be surmounted since the likely alternative is a steady escalation toward more crises.

Thank you.

[The prepared statement of Mr. Swaine follows:]

CARNEGIE
ENDOWMENT FOR
INTERNATIONAL PEACE

Congressional Testimony

CHECKING CHINA'S MARITIME PUSH

Testimony by **Michael D. Swaine**
Senior Fellow, Asia Program
Carnegie Endowment for International Peace

Testimony before the House Foreign Affairs
Committee

February 28, 2017

Thank you very much Mr. Chairman.

Since roughly 2007–2008, the People's Republic of China has clearly taken a more active, assertive stance toward its longstanding territorial claims in the South China Sea (SCS) and East China Sea (ECS), both bordering its long maritime coast. Such activities have included, among others:

- Strong statements criticizing the actions and claims of other disputants, especially Japan (in the East China Sea) and Vietnam and the Philippines (in the South China Sea)
- The establishment of new administrative authorities charged with managing various aspects of the claimed land and sea features
- The increased use of military and especially para-military air and naval assets to challenge the activities of other claimants in disputed areas, and sometimes even in what are generally regarded as "open ocean" areas or within the exclusive economic zones of other nations
- The establishment of an air defense identification zone over the East China Sea that includes disputed territories with Japan
- The creation of artificial islands in the Spratly Islands and the deployment of air defense weapons systems and the construction of dual-use civilian-military facilities on those islands

While not taking any formal position in support of any claimant's sovereignty position, Washington has clearly focused the vast majority of its concern, and its actions since roughly 2010, on Beijing. This has led many in China to conclude that the United States is actively supporting the other disputants while attempting to undermine China's position and influence in the disputed areas.

The obvious danger presented by this situation is that increasing numbers of U.S. and Chinese air and naval assets operating in close proximity to one another, or perceived provocations of various sorts including further military deployments onto islands or rocks or possible clashes between China and other disputants, could produce escalating crises. These might draw the United States into direct confrontation with Beijing, as the latter acts excessively to strengthen its position and thereby deter or counter perceived provocations (perhaps out of an exaggerated sense of its growing power) and the former overreacts to such a perceived challenge in an effort to reaffirm its predominant position and maintain its credibility as a security guarantor.

This danger is reinforced by the absence of any serious dialogue among the claimants and between the United States and China regarding limits on the level and type of militarization occurring in disputed maritime areas, and the failure of China—and to a lesser extent other disputants—to clarify their specific claims regarding various waters, particularly in the South China Sea. Contrary to widespread claims in the media, Beijing has yet to define exactly what the so-called Nine-Dashed-Line denotes regarding the waters within it.

The resulting uncertainties stimulate worst casing about motives and behavior, thus leading to further escalation. And of course the fact that sovereignty issues are generally zero-sum in nature and elicit strong nationalist emotions further adds to the dangers.

Managing this complex and potentially volatile issue requires a clear understanding of the stakes involved for all sides (both now and in the future), the likely foundations of long-term stability, and the probable resources available to the United States to manage this issue.

Maritime Motives and Stakes

China's ultimate motives in expanding its influence and presence in nearby disputed maritime areas are not entirely clear, despite what some observers argue is a clear effort to "control" these areas and push the United States out of East Asia.

In truth, the historical dynamic at work in the disputed maritime areas has long involved an interactive tit-for-tat rivalry among the claimants, made possible by the absence of any clear and commonly accepted code of conduct (beyond the voluntary, nonbinding, and vague 2002 Declaration on the Conduct of Parties in the South China Sea signed between China and ASEAN) and driven by deep-seated suspicions and strongly felt nationalist impulses on all sides.

In the South China Sea competition (which focuses mainly on the southern Spratly Islands since China has firmly held the northern Paracel Islands for many years), Beijing is by far the biggest player. There, it is seeking to use its growing capabilities to more effectively defend and advance what it regards as its indisputable claims to the land features and undefined adjoining waters of the area, as well as certain also undefined historical rights. Other claimants are doing virtually the same thing, except their capabilities and claims are not as extensive, their actions not as effective, and hence their activities do not generate as much attention. In general, they are hopelessly outmatched by Beijing in this competition.

In recent years, however, Beijing has certainly gone beyond a proportional tit-for-tat interaction to apparent attempts to establish itself as the dominant claimant in the Spratly Islands, arguably to deter future perceived provocations by others and to establish a strong position in future negotiations. This impulse is driven even further by the fact that Beijing has historically held a very weak position in that area compared with Vietnam, the other claimant to virtually all the land features within the South China Sea.

In the case of the East China Sea dispute with Japan, Beijing has also departed from its past basic tit-for-tat stance in an attempt to establish itself in recent years as an equal claimant to Tokyo over the Senkaku/Diaoyu Islands, thereby supposedly correcting years of Japanese dominance.

Regardless of its motives, China's more recent, escalatory behavior has contributed significantly to the buildup in tensions in the disputed maritime areas. At the same time, when measured against the metric of a supposed direct challenge to the U.S. position in Asia, Beijing's actions appear at least somewhat cautious. It generally avoids the use of warships to assert its claims, has given assurances that it does not intend to militarize the Spratly Islands beyond the placement of what it calls "defensive capabilities," and has certainly not attempted to seize land features long held by other claimants to assure its control of the area.

Moreover, Beijing continues to insist that it is dedicated to a peaceful, negotiated solution of the disputes and supports the peaceful objectives of the 2002 declaration. Most recently, it has supported reaching a basic framework for a more detailed Code of Conduct by mid-2017. In general, one can say that it is attempting to increase its influence in both seas without greatly increasing the chance of armed conflict with the United States or other claimants.

This could change, of course, as China's power and presence in the area increase. Those in and out of the U.S. Government who call for a zero-sum confrontation with Beijing over the maritime disputes assert that it certainly will, allegedly because China's caution thus far conceals its "real" expansionist and aggressive motives.

This is pure speculation, but of a dangerous sort, since if accepted as a basis for U.S. policy it would basically lock in a zero-sum interpretation of every assertive Chinese action, thereby justifying an equally zero-sum U.S. move in response. And of course, such actions would indeed cause Beijing to eventually adopt precisely the threatening motives that some observers insist (in my view incorrectly) are already present.

Relative Capabilities

Beyond basing itself on a purely speculative and dangerous set of assumptions about Chinese motives, a zero-sum, confrontational argument calling for a doubling down of U.S. capabilities in the Western Pacific also employs another highly dubious (at best) set of assumptions regarding American and Chinese defense spending relevant to Asia.

Barring an unlikely near-total collapse of the Chinese economy and/or a major surge in the overall U.S. GDP, Washington will not possess the capacity to greatly exceed the kind of military and economic capabilities that China will be able to bring to bear in its nearby maritime areas over the coming years.

In fact, projections by myself and other scholars at the Carnegie Endowment for International Peace, along with other reputable sources, predict a much more likely movement toward parity between U.S. and Chinese capabilities in that region, in other words, a de facto strategic equilibrium or balance of power.[1]

Of course, the United States could devote a much larger share of its available economic resources to defense spending, and to spending in Asia in particular, in an attempt to remain clearly dominant militarily in the Western Pacific near China. However, that would likely require either considerable belt-tightening elsewhere, especially in vital social welfare or entitlement areas, or a huge expansion in the government deficit. Neither of these is politically feasible at present or for the foreseeable future, absent a truly major increase in public perceptions of the threat posed by China.

Disputes over rocks and islands in the far reaches of Asia are unlikely to motivate such a level of alarm, unless a crisis in that region escalates to a genuine Sino-U.S. military clash of serious proportions. While certainly possible, such a hypothetical crisis should not be assumed and likely could not a priori alter threat perceptions.

The Most Feasible and Viable Way Forward

The complexity of the maritime disputes in the East and South China Seas, involving a) economic resources; b) differing interpretations of applicable international law and historical rights; c)

---

[1] For details, see Michael D. Swaine with Wenyan Deng and Aube Rey Lescure, *Creating a Stable Asia: An Agenda for a U.S.-China Balance of Power*, Carnegie Endowment for International Peace, Washington D.C., 2016.

overlapping jurisdictional claims based on continental shelves, exclusive economic zones, and other relevant legal zones; and d) domestic political factors rooted in strong nationalist sentiments, together suggest that any resolution, if at all possible, will take many years, and perhaps decades, to achieve.

In the meantime, a stable, enduring modus vivendi among all relevant parties is needed, centered on mutual restraint in asserting local sovereign or special rights as well as an effective, peaceful process for handling incidents.

Such an understanding ideally should consist of several elements. The first is an initial shift away from military and para-military competition and maneuvering toward an emphasis on diplomacy, primarily via an initial set of interim (short- to medium-term) understandings among the claimants and between Beijing and Washington regarding levels and types of militarization and the non-use of force. This must be based on clear, agreed-upon definitions of acceptable and unacceptable military behavior and clear, specific proscriptions on the unprovoked display and use of force.

As a part of this negotiation process, some level of mutually acceptable long-term equilibrium in the military capabilities of the claimants within the Spratly archipelago in particular must be achieved, as a stable ceiling against future militarization. This might involve permission for claimants other than China (such as Vietnam) to upgrade or expand their facilities on land features in the Spratly Islands to bring them up to a par with those that Beijing has constructed.

Without such an understanding, any transition toward diplomatic efforts on claims, jurisdictions, resource development, and an eventual long-term code of conduct for both the East China and South China Seas will remain virtually impossible, as all sides continue to maneuver militarily to deter one another.

The United States and China must take the lead in this effort, based on a common recognition of the need to remove the maritime issue as a driver of their deepening strategic contention. That said, a Chinese acceptance of such limits would doubtless prove conditional, based on the eventual acceptance by the other claimants.

Such agreements will require overcoming domestic military and paramilitary resistance to any restraints on military activities in disputed areas, including limits on the frequency of Freedom of Navigation (FON) operations by the U.S. Navy. They also require overcoming the argument that any agreement to eschew an unprovoked use of force would undermine the sovereignty claims of China and the other claimants.

Second, a staged diplomatic process is necessary for clarifying the precise content and legal or other rationale of the many claims involved, that is, the jurisdictional disputes involving both sovereignty issues and non-sovereignty (but privileged) rights over resource extraction, such as fishing. Washington should do more to facilitate this effort.

This could proceed on a bilateral or multilateral basis but should gradually expand to eventually include all extant claims across the East China and South China Seas. During this process, Beijing would need to clarify the meaning of the nine-dash line, and all claimants would specify their claims to land or underwater features and corresponding waters as they relate to relevant legal (that is, based on the United Nations Convention on the Law of the Sea) definitions, as well as so-called historical rights. When the status of specific features (as islands, rocks, reefs, and so on) is clearly in dispute, the parties concerned must negotiate a compromise or petition for a ruling from the International Tribunal for the Law of the Sea (ITLOS) under UNCLOS.

Third, on the basis of such clarification of claims and jurisdiction, all parties must reach an agreement on those areas subject to joint resource development and a procedure for implementing such development. Although often called for, joint development cannot actually occur unless all disputants clarify those areas that are subject to such development, and this cannot occur until the specific areas of overlapping claims are identified and agreed upon.

In principle, joint development of disputed maritime areas is already accepted by most if not all disputants as a valid interim means of exploiting resources before any resolution of claims, although some compromise and agreement on the division of proceeds is required. Hence an agreement on such development, once the areas of overlapping claims have been identified, should not prove excessively difficult to achieve.

Fourth, on the basis of the previous actions, the claimants must eventually negotiate elements of a binding code of conduct for limiting levels of militarization and handling future incidents over the long term. This code must build on: a) previously agreed-upon, clear definitions of prohibited activities of all kinds, military and nonmilitary alike (the existing 2002 Declaration on the Conduct of Parties in the South China Sea is extremely vague on this point); b) a process for identifying and interpreting such activities; and c) a means of punishing violations.

Some observers might argue that the formulation of a binding code of conduct should precede these steps, as a necessary precondition. However, it is almost certainly the case that the willingness of highly assertive states locked in contentious sovereignty disputes to agree confidently to a binding code will require a prior increased level of trust, a reduced propensity for military competition, and a clear understanding of the nature and extent of competing claims that can only result from the above steps.

Obviously, many obstacles would confront any efforts to greatly reduce disputes over maritime territorial claims as a source of Sino-U.S. tension or conflict, including distrust among virtually all the parties concerned, nationalist domestic pressures, and deeply entrenched bureaucratic interests. And American leverage is extremely limited by its failure to ratify UNCLOS. How can Washington seriously press China and others to abide by UNCLOS rulings and establish a Code of Conduct when it refuses to subject itself to such scrutiny? In addition, more extensive confidence-building measures (CBMs) and crisis management mechanisms (CMMs) are also likely to constitute necessary preconditions, to reduce distrust and strengthen confidence in the enforceability of a legally binding code of conduct.

On the U.S. side, political leaders will also need to reassure Manila and especially Tokyo that any agreement Washington makes with Beijing to limit the content or scope of its military activities in disputed areas will not place those countries at a disadvantage either militarily or with regard to sovereignty claims.

U.S. leaders will also need to clarify what constitutes unacceptable coercion or intimidation. Not all forms of Chinese assertiveness would necessarily threaten the U.S. interest in a stable and peaceful environment. Similarly, on the Chinese side, limits on the use or display of force and clarifications of existing claims will require, on both sides, a determined and strong leadership able to manage backlashes by nationalists and the military and a clear sense of what constitutes unacceptable coercion.

In sum, the only effective way to create a more stable environment in the maritime areas near China is for the United States to lead a serious diplomatic dialogue with Beijing and other claimants aimed at establishing mutually acceptable restraints, accompanied by strong U.S. and allied deterrence signals, ideally as part of a larger effort to create a regional balance of power. Such deterrence signals should involve clear indications of the adverse consequences for China (and for regional stability) that would result from a failure to reach an agreement. A unilateral, near-term doubling down on military deployments, a drastic increase in defense assistance to those powers opposing China, or a drawing of high stakes "lines in the sand" directed at Beijing on their own will not achieve this objective and could make the situation much worse.

———

Mr. YOHO. Thank you. And I appreciate everybody's comments. And that is what we are here for, you know, let's define the region. Let's define what the norms are.

Dr. Auslin, you were talking about China pressing its national sovereignty in the out islands against international norms. Our historical agreements with countries like Japan, the Philippines, Taiwan, South Korea, if we look at the advent of those when they came out, it was peaceful in nature, non-aggressive, and non-encroaching on other nations whereas what we are seeing with the Government of China has expanded its reach. We see the militarization of the islands that have come out of nowhere, the castles in the sand. And I think your description of the lake of China versus the South and East China Sea is very descriptive in the mentality coming from the Chinese Government.

When we see the—not just offensive weapons on there—or the defensive but the offensive weapons, I think it is time that we come to the table and get clarification on this so that we can make policies and get people in agreement on that.

After becoming party chairman in the late 2012, President Xi announced his so-called Chinese dream, which he said would lead to the great rejuvenation of the Chinese nation. How important do you think China's maritime claim in the South and East China Seas are to achieving President Xi's Chinese dream? That is question number one.

What is Beijing's ultimate goal in the South and East China Seas, and how far do you believe China is willing to go to defend these claims? And I am going to open it up to all three of you, but Dr. Auslin, if you will start on that.

Mr. AUSLIN. Thank you, Mr. Chairman.

I think that, in terms of the ultimate goal that Xi Jinping has, it is—which is not surprising for any national leader—it is to have the ability to do what he decides he wants to do in the future, meaning, to reduce any restrictions on either his own capabilities, which is a domestic issue, or against those, such as the United States, who may pose an obstacle, or potentially international norms that conflict with those interests.

One thing I don't think we have fully appreciated here in the States is the degree to which China considers the new territories that it has built and reclaimed in the South China Sea as sovereign territory and how that will change Chinese doctrine, military doctrine, defense doctrine should they feel that those territories are at risk. After all, they point out to us that those are—there are post offices and schools on the islands, not just airstrips and defensive installations.

I think, secondly, to wind up in terms of your question as to how important this is, it is—I would not say it is the single most important driver of China's perception of its own position and role in the region, but it is part of a much larger perception that China has of regaining a position of dominance that it once had, of being recognized as, if not the hegemon, as the dominant player, and, therefore, with the ability to have its own perceptions of what its interests are and the norms that surround those respected by its neighbors.

This is where the other nations and Asia push back. It is where the United States has hesitated to step in to uphold the global norms that go on to issues that include free trade and fair trade. So that is where I would actually link Ranking Member Sherman's opening statement with our discussion on security. It is a question of liberal norms and behavior globally.

Thank you.

Mr. YOHO. All right. Let me interject in here.

Dr. Swaine, you were saying, as you stated, it will be harder in the future for us to have more of a presence there. You know, if you look at our economic situation and our military strength, that is why I find it is imperative that we have an agreement now and understanding that we can build from in the future. What are your thoughts on the direction that we should go and knowing our current state of affairs in America?

Mr. SWAINE. Oh, that is an important caveat.

Mr. YOHO. We will just deal with the Asia-Pacific area right now.

Mr. SWAINE. Yes. I mean, in some respects I think we are moving in the wrong direction on a lot of fronts.

Mr. YOHO. Agreed.

Mr. SWAINE. I am not a big fan of the revoking of TPP. I think it can be modified, and it is something that signifies American's presence in the area. But I do believe that it is incumbent on the United States to think long term on this issue and think hard about what our relative capabilities in that field, in that area, because they are changing. And the ability of the United States to be able to predominate in the Western Pacific is going to go away. And so how do you deal with that effectively? Well, you can argue that you want to double down and just spend more on defense, and you will maintain that gap. I don't think that is going to be feasible, particularly if the United States is not a strong economic player in the region as well.

So the best procedure is to move toward some type of balance of power in the region. And that means gaining understandings with, first of all, allies, the United States with Japan, with South Korea, and with the Philippines, about what is needed in the region in the long term. And, secondly, reassuring them that balance of power does not mean accommodation. Balance of power does not mean retreat from the region. Balance of power does not mean a weak U.S. The U.S. acts on the basis of its strength and influence to try to do that.

And I have laid out a whole series of moves that I think are necessary in a report that I wrote last year on this question.

Mr. YOHO. I saw that. And I appreciate that because that is what this is all about. You know, we can't do it. It is not sustainable for us to do it alone. We have to come to agreements in that area so that we can forge strong alliances and have a common understanding because if we allow the precedent of China moving on, does that allow any other nation to do the same thing?

Mr. SWAINE. Right.

Mr. YOHO. And that is what I fear. We need to come together on an agreement.

I am out of time, and I am going to turn this over to the ranking member for his 5 minutes.

Mr. SHERMAN. Thank you. I want to make it clear: I regard this aggressiveness by China as important. I am just not so sure it is as important as the administration has said as ISIS or Crimea.

American weakness is hurting us, and American weakness is demonstrated by our weakness on trade, and our response is, well, let's get tough on the islands. Yes, China may be stealing some fish from Japan, but China's refusal to accept American imports, China's demand for coproduction agreements, where we have to transfer technology as a price for access to their markets, this has devastated Michigan and Wisconsin and Ohio and western Pennsylvania, millions of American families, and we show weakness every day that we do not impose tariffs on Chinese goods coming into our country.

And the best way to preserve our weakness is to say: Look over here. There are some islands. There are some fish.

What we haven't discussed much here is how China and its government can use nationalism to expand power. It works here; it works there. Now, the Chinese Government has a problem in that there is no theoretical answer for the question, why does that government rule? Democracy is a good theoretical basis. Theocracy works reasonably well for the government of Tehran, and even the divine right of kings has justified why people are in control. But the rulers in Beijing are not the vanguard of the proletariat.

Their only answer for the question why they rule is the exaggerated nationalism, and we play right into that hand. We may have to because they may get so aggressive that we have to respond. But we play right into their hands when we confront them in the South China Sea.

Dr. Auslin, you talk about coercive diplomacy. Do you have anything in mind other than yelling loud? Give me—spend 10 seconds and just tell me what is—one example of coercive diplomacy.

Mr. AUSLIN [continuing]. Including disinviting China from maritime exercises we can invite them to like RIMPAC, curtailing military exchanges, considering whether or not to continue high-level diplomatic dialogue.

Mr. SHERMAN. Some of that just makes the South China Sea far more dangerous. They play games; we respond. And I don't want to start a war there by accident. I notice, of course, you didn't say tariffs as part of that.

You say that $1.2 trillion of U.S. trade passes through the South China Sea. Can you name the number one port that that trade goes to that isn't Chinese? Is any significant portion of that $1.2 trillion not U.S. trade with China?

Mr. AUSLIN. All the leading ports are Chinese.

Mr. SHERMAN. All the leading ports are Chinese. So, once again, these strategic islands would allow China to close off trade with the United States through Chinese ports.

Dr. Swaine, Japan has this constitutional provision. Does that prevent them from spending 1.5 percent of their GDP or even 2 percent of their GDP on defense? Does that prevent them from defending what they say is their own territory?

Mr. SWAINE. Well, by law, they have restrictions on the amount that they pay as a percentage of their GDP——

Mr. SHERMAN. That is by law. That is not their constitution. We have a law that we spend only so much for defense, but we change that every year.

Mr. SWAINE. They could spend more.

Mr. SHERMAN. And they could spend more. They could, and they choose not to because they would rather we defend them——

Mr. SWAINE. Well, if I may, it is a little bit more complicated than that.

Mr. SHERMAN. I am sure it is. And if I was given more than 5 minutes, we would explore those complications. And, again, we respect the Japanese people, but their willingness to tax themselves to defend what they claim is their sovereign territory faces certain political limits, and we are told that we have got to increase our defense budget by 10 percent and that these islands are an important part of that.

And 9/11 happened 16 years ago. Has there been any effort in Japan to say we have to amend our constitution so that we can send forces to Afghanistan?

Dr. Auslin, name the leading Japanese politician who has called for the deployment of Japanese troops to Afghanistan?

Mr. AUSLIN. Combat troops, none, but they sent reconstruction troops to Afghanistan. And they had an 8-year refueling mis- sion——

Mr. SHERMAN. Okay. But they haven't put their people in harm's way?

Mr. AUSLIN. They are precluded by the constitution——

Mr. SHERMAN. And not a single Japanese politician has stood up and said: "America has defended us for the better part of a century. America was attacked on 9/11. It is time for us to change our constitution for the purpose of helping America." No Japanese politician has said that?

Mr. AUSLIN. Congressman, they respond to their constituents as you do.

Mr. SHERMAN. Exactly. And their constituents want my constituents to pay for the defense of their islands, and their constituents don't want to pay in blood or treasure for the defense of America, which is happening in Afghanistan right now.

Again, these islands are important. We shouldn't let China walk all over us, but the other view I am glad to have represented here. And I think we have a balanced hearing because I am sure that there will be others who will present the other side.

I yield back.

Mr. ROHRABACHER [presiding]. Well, thank you.

And I would yield to myself while the chairman is out. Look at that. I have got it in my hands finally.

Mr. SHERMAN. Wait a minute. You have got one on your—you are controlling the whole world.

Mr. ROHRABACHER. That is it. There you go.

I have some very strong agreements with Mr. Sherman on some of the trade issues that he has brought up today, and I also have some very strong disagreements with him as to the scope and depth of how we approach China today, a threatening China to the world peace.

Certainly, China—I led the floor fight when I came here with Chris Cox against Most Favored Nation status with China. At that time, we made the argument that those people were telling us that the more fluent and the more trade—the more fluent China with more trade in the United States meant a liberalization of China, that we would eventually have a more democratic government. That has proven to be absolutely wrong. And I call it the "hug a Nazi, make a liberal" theory. And it is no more, liberal and politically, than it was two decades or three decades. In fact, there is some evidence that, at that time, because of Tiananmen Square, they actually had more freedom than they have today in terms of political freedom in China.

So let us note that the idea that we have permitted a monstrously oppressive regime that brutalizes their own people, that we have enabled them to put the rules of trade together that has resulted in a massive transfer of wealth that has then been kept in the control of the clique that runs China—and as you said, Mr. Sherman, this is not a clique that is now directed by beliefs of some philosophy like they are the proletariat, as they were during the Communist days. This is just a self-serving, vicious, fascist-state clique that runs China, and that threatens the world when that type of clique becomes a massive military power and dominates a region of the world. That is when it becomes a threat beyond trade. And that is what is happening today.

That massive wealth is being used to build up their military capabilities, and what we have seen is an arrogance of decision-making in Beijing, and I would say, again, there are no opposition parties there. There are no people—there is no reason for them to worry about public opinion. This is just a power play by arrogant oppressors, as we have seen in many throughout history. You have a vicious dictatorship in a country that becomes a military power. They always end up aggressing upon their neighbors.

So, with that, that means we have a threat to deal with, especially when all the signs are there, which in the South China Sea is not a—if I can just note here, the South China Sea is closer, the Spratly Islands and these other islands here, maybe not the Paracels, but the islands—the Paracel Islands—are closer to the other countries in the South China Sea, meaning the Philippines and even Indonesia and certainly Vietnam, are much closer to those countries than they are to China. There was no island there before. We are talking about reefs that were under water at high water.

Now, I was lucky, after the CIA for decades prevented me—I should say for a decade, not decades—for a decade prevented me from flying over the Spratly Islands. And about 15 years ago, I managed to fly—get another plane from another—anywhere where I got it, to fly me over the Spratly Islands. And there they were building the islands. And so all of this time for the last 15 years, we know that they have been building those islands, and we have let it happen. We have not confronted it, which they have seen as a sign of weakness.

And what maybe we could have done, maybe start building islands of our own. We could have maybe financed the Filipinos to go there and build their own islands right next door, see what they would have thought about that. But most importantly. And we are trying to come to this formula, and I have only got a couple of minutes for you to reply, but let me just note: I think the most important thing in making sure that we have peace and stability in that part of the world is not to ignore everything but the trade with China, but make sure that we work with the Japanese. The Japanese are the only ones who are strong enough to counterbalance this.

And let me note that if the United States had had a country foolish enough for decades to say, "Let us take care of all of your defense," the American people wouldn't be in favor of using their money when the other country would let them cover their defense. It is time for us not to cover the defense of Japan but treat the Japanese as equal partners and allies and help President Abe, who is committed to being a force to counteract this what I consider to be evil coming out of Beijing.

Now, I have overspoke my time, but I will give all you witnesses 15 seconds to say "you are out of your mind" or "I really like what you had to say."

Mr. CHENG. I would note, sir, that what is essential is a comprehensive approach toward dealing with China. We cannot succeed in dealing with China simply via trade or simply via military or simply via diplomatic issues. Comprehensive includes what you have noted, which is working with our allies, but it also means thinking about all of the instruments available to the United States, including access to our markets, as Representative Sherman has suggested, including financial markets as well as things like supply chains and things like that where many—much of that trade is going to China. That is not finished products necessarily, but it is often key spare parts.

Mr. ROHRABACHER. Very good.

Mr. AUSLIN. Representative, just very briefly, I think we do start with our allies and partners. Japan spends $50 billion on its military per year. It is purchasing advanced weaponry, such as the F-35, and it does take the lead in protecting its own islands in the Senkakus. The United States Navy has done none of that. What they have asked for is a guarantee that, should war break out with China, that we would honor our alliance commitment to them. But the Japanese Coast Guard and Navy are always the first responders constantly to China.

Mr. SWAINE. You are out of your mind. No.

Mr. ROHRABACHER. Great.

Mr. SWAINE. I mean, I just fundamentally disagree with many, many of your assumptions, Congressman.

Mr. ROHRABACHER. Okay.

Mr. SWAINE. I mean, I think looking at the Chinese system as simply a question of Communist dictators bent on overtaking the world is a very inaccurate way of understanding them. Yes, it is a one-party dictatorship. Yes, they restrict a lot of political freedoms within their regime. They are not, however, ruling over a population that is dying to overthrow them. They have a lot of people in China who are very supportive of what the PRC regime has done over the last 30 to 40 years, and I am sure you are aware of that. It has raised their standards of living up very, very high.

No, they don't have political rights in a variety of ways that we would like them to have, but they are not going to become like an American liberal democracy. They are going to have some version of some kind of stronger state because of the size of the country and because of the history of the country and the fear that they have had of instability and collapse within that regime.

Now, you can argue that a democratic China would be much better for us and much better for them, but give me a good sense about how you get there without creating chaos, and I would be very willing to hear because nobody has thought of how to do this. So what you have, then, is an effort on the part of the Chinese Government to expand their growth as great as they can, and they do it for the people as well as for themselves, and to establish a military that is going to reduce what they regard as their vulnerabilities.

The United States has dominated the Western Pacific right up to China's 12-mile limit for the last 70 years. That is changing. The question is, how do you address that problem without provoking a conflict with the Chinese?

They are not like Iraq. They are not like Granada. They are not like Panama. They have nuclear weapons and a big military.

Mr. ROHRABACHER. All right. Thank you.

And we do have fundamental disagreements, but neither one of us are out of our mind. So we will have a good discussion on that. Thank you.

And Mr. Becerra.

Mr. BERA. Mr. Bera. Mr. Becerra is back in California.

Mr. ROHRABACHER. No, we just met with him this afternoon.

Mr. BERA. You know, I think this is a very important and interesting dialogue. I would agree with you, Dr. Auslin, that as we look at Asia and the Pacific, and certainly East Asia, in the latter half of the 20th century, post World War II, post the Korean conflict, the U.S. presence really did have a remarkable effect in creating a stable democracy in Japan, creating a stable democracy in the Republic of Korea, you know, helping create thriving economies. And that was a good thing.

And I do think it is important for us to reassure our allies in the region that we are not withdrawing from the region. I think it is also a good thing as Prime Minister Abe and the Japanese Government looks at stepping up some of its own defensive capabilities, understanding some of the threats.

And one of those threats, clearly, are tensions in the South China Sea. And I would agree with my colleague, Mr. Rohrabacher, that we should have responded sooner, but we are where we are. And part of the challenge of not responding sooner is there is—if you look at some of the Chinese strategy is they will provoke, see what kind of response that they get. If they don't get a response, well, then they will push a little bit further and see what kind of response. And at this juncture, it becomes a much more complicated issue, much more so in the South China Sea than in the East China Sea.

None of us has an interest in creating a kinetic conflict. And there is always a danger of an accidental kinetic conflict, which whether that is a Chinese vessel with a Japanese vessel or a Filipino vessel or an American vessel. And that is the danger. So we do have to think about strategies to start reducing those tensions. I do think, you know, the other big piece of it, whether you sup- ported TPP or were opposed to TPP, these are the fastest growing markets in the world. There clearly is a benefit to American com- panies to be able to compete and sell in these markets. You know, we sell a lot of American products in Japan. We sell a lot of Amer- ican products in Korea. And as the other southeast Asian markets and Chinese markets open up, we want to be able to compete and sell our products there. That is good for American workers. We want to make sure we do it in a fair way.

If I start to think about the next steps—and maybe I will give each of you a chance to talk about that—with this desire to avoid a kinetic conflict, that wouldn't be in China's interests, either. What would be one or two next steps to start reducing those ten- sions, and using some of our soft power to reduce and deescalate the region?

Maybe, Mr. Cheng, if you want to start.

Mr. CHENG. Thank you very much, Representative.

Several thoughts do come to mind. First, I think it is very impor- tant to note that the Chinese leadership does have to worry about public opinion. They are not subject to election, of course, but when we watch how quickly they suppress and limit the internet and the free flow of information, it is very clear, that is something that worries them.

And that is something that we should continue to champion at a political level, internet freedom; at a governance level, in terms of not walking away from things like ICANN; and at a technical level, in terms of promoting the ability to flow information around, over, and through the Great Firewall of China.

The other thing here is to consider the extent to which China's activities in places like the South China Sea land reclamation are, nonetheless, dependent on Chinese companies, which, in turn, are dependent upon imports. The spare parts required for the mechan- ical act of reclamation often is sourced not in China, ironically enough, but in Europe or the United States. And a diplomatic effort on the part of the U.S. to bring in Japan and our allies, to basically constrain Chinese behavior, or else suffer the consequences to their supply chains, is, I think, one that is worth considering.

Mr. BERA. Dr. Auslin.

Mr. AUSLIN. Congressman, I think you are right, that we are where we are, meaning we are in a different situation today than we were 8 years ago, or 16 years ago. There are certain things we cannot do today. There are other things that we can.

I would say, first, we do need to consider how to best build the capacity of our partners, high-end partners such as Japan as well as lower-end partners, those that are struggling to just protect their own waterways.

Second, I think enhancing the U.S. presence, ensuring that we maintain a robust, U.S. presence, which is both air and ground and naval in the region, that there is co-training, there are exercises, there are port visits and the like, is not inherently predominance, but it does maintain stability and it sends messages of reassurance.

At best, what I think we want—not at best, what I think we want to do is complicate China's perception of what it is able to do uncontested in these areas, and nudge it toward a more cooperative posture. And I think you do that by creating a community of interests.

Mr. BERA. Dr. Swaine.

Mr. SWAINE. Well, I mean, there are several different aspects to what needs to be done. One of them is domestic. The United States needs to, as I said before, think very carefully about what the long-range future of the United States is in the Western Pacific, in terms of its capabilities, its influence, how likely is it able to match specific types of resources with specific types of objectives.

And I don't think that dialogue or that discussion has occurred. Nobody thinks really long term about U.S. capabilities and tries to understand a range of outcomes that may occur and what you would do to try and minimize the less likely, or the less favorable ones and maximize the more favorable ones. That is the first thing.

The second thing I think we have to do is we have to have a discussion with our allies about them improving their relations in various ways with the Chinese. There is very little discussion by the United States in interacting with China and ASEAN to do with their disputes in the South China Sea. After all, the disputes are about them; it is about their relationships. And we need to be more effective diplomatically and not be reducing the State Department, cutting back on the State Department's capability, in order to engage with allies and with others in the region on how they are going to develop a real code of conduct.

The Chinese have committed themselves to this. They are supposed to have a framework for a code of conduct by the middle of this year. The United States barely says a thing about it. It needs to base itself on the 2002 declaration that ASEAN and China reached, and then use that as a basis for moving forward for a code of conduct that will cover a lot of these areas.

Mr. BERA. Thank you.

Mr. YOHO [presiding]. Thank you. I am going to afford Mr. Sherman 30 seconds.

Mr. SHERMAN. One comment is that we might be stronger diplomatically if we were part of UNCLOS. We don't subscribe to the international standards for maritime disputes, but we demand China do so.

But I want to pick up on what Mr. Cheng said. They do need to manipulate their domestic public opinion. They will especially need to do that if economic conditions change, and they can no longer, you know, provide 5 or 10 percent economic growth. And if there is a recession in China, the best, or the most likely way for them to try to retain power is to go eyeball to eyeball with us and wrap themselves in nationalism.

I yield back.

Mr. YOHO. Thank you. At this time, we will go to Mr. Perry from Pennsylvania.

Mr. PERRY. Thanks, Mr. Chairman.

I know this goes back a ways. It is probably longer than most people care to think about, and maybe it is not even relevant to today's conversation. But I would think, for historical purposes, it is important that we remind ourselves in a way how we got here. And I am one of the people that believes that a United States diplomat named John Service in the fall of Chiang Kai-Shek as opposed to Mao and our State Department and our meddling on behalf of communists have helped create the problem that we now find ourselves within. And I just think it is important to think about those things, because I see parallels to today with some other places we are engaged and other things we are doing.

That having been said, I turn to Mr. Cheng. Our new Secretary of State Tillerson warned of a more confrontational South China Sea policy, but he also said that the island building had to stop, and that access to those islands would not be allowed.

The President has recognized the one China policy, as we all know. The last administration expressed a floor for China, including the militarization of the South China Sea; but as far as I can tell, that was never backed up, never backed up with any action.

So the question is, so if we are going to maintain, if we are going to maintain that there is a floor for China, what specific conditions should we articulate to China regarding that; and when China invariably breaks the floor, or floors, what should our actions be?

Mr. CHENG. Congressman, I think that, to begin with, we should be treating our allies and our friends at least as well as we treat China. So I think that the incorporation of China into things like RIMPAC, when forces from, for example, the Republic of China/Taiwan are excluded sends, I think, a very distinct message to Beijing, especially when they show up not only with the forces that are supposed to show up, but also spy ships which were uninvited.

And yet, we are apparently going to invite them yet again. They showed up in 2014 with a spy ship as well as their forces. They showed up in 2016. And now, apparently, we are going to invite them again in 2018. That isn't even a floor; that is not a net; that is an open doorway.

I think that, with regards to confrontation, again, there are economic aspects that can be undertaken. The companies that are doing this reclamation should be given a fairly simple choice. You can work for China and make millions, or you can work the global market that the U.S., Europe, and Japan can influence, and that is billions of dollars. I think many of these companies may well, at least, impose pressure on their own system to rethink some of their policies.

And then with regards to our allies, again, I think that many of them are still militarily less capable. They want to cooperate with the United States. We are representing the gold standard. That doesn't mean we shouldn't be engaging diplomatically. It doesn't mean we shouldn't be engaging in other aspects. But these are things that also do send a political signal as well, whether it is sales of more advanced weapons, or whether it is cooperating in—inviting our friends and allies to cooperate in multinational military exercises.

Mr. PERRY. So that seems pretty proactive, I mean, not inviting the Chinese. Maybe we continue to invite them, but we also invite our allies is what you are saying. But I would say that there also should be an immediate prohibition of them bringing the spy ship, if you want to call it that. Right? That seems pretty axiomatic as well as making the contractors make a choice. Right? That seems pretty obvious as well. But those are kind of prospective, right? We could make that decision right now.

But anticipating that China will always step one foot closer, what is in our arsenal of diplomatic—and maybe "arsenal" is not the right term, right, but what is in our grab bag of options, something that will be meaningful to China when it is either imposed upon them or taken away from them, et cetera?

Mr. CHENG. Congressman, I think that, again, access to our markets is something that China wants as much as we want access to theirs. Financial markets in particular. We, in an odd way, represent sort of the underwriters limited seal of approval when a Chinese IPO occurs.

And the inability to access our stock markets, our financial networks, is something that should be undertaken very carefully, because that is a very, very serious step, but it does send a very serious message to Beijing. If you want to still benefit from that global transfer of funds that undergirds your economy, then you need to play by the rules, the rules that you have already signed up to play by.

Mr. PERRY. Always a privilege, Mr. Cheng.

Thank you, Mr. Chairman.

Mr. YOHO. Thank you. And now we will go to Ms. Titus from Nevada.

Ms. TITUS. Thank you, Mr. Chairman.

Perhaps we shouldn't have been so anxious to send Bao Bao back if we are facing these kind of diplomatic problems.

All of you have mentioned that we need to increase our engagement in the South China Sea, and all of you have mentioned we need to do this through diplomacy, not just with China, but with our other allies there. You pointed that out, Mr. Cheng.

Dr. Auslin said, I think your quote was energetic diplomacy through ASEAN, or attending some of these other summits.

And then Dr. Swaine, you noted the only effective way to create a more stable environment in the maritime areas near China is for the U.S. to lead a serious diplomatic dialogue with Beijing and others in the area. You kind of trumped my question there in passing in your earlier answer, but I would like to hear all of you say, how in the world are we going to be able to increase diplomacy, not just with China, but the other areas, when we have no clear message coming out of the White House? We have so many vacancies at top levels in the State Department, and we have what we anticipate a budget from this new President where they are just cutting as much as they can from the State Department.

How are we not creating a power vacuum there? How are we going to deal with this situation? Maybe, Dr. Swaine, you could start.

Mr. SWAINE. Well, you are preaching to the choir on this. I think what is—we don't know yet, right, exactly what the Trump administration intends to do by way of cutting back in order to pay for a $54 billion increase in defense spending. It is claiming that it is going to have offsets to be able to do this without having to raise taxes or increase the deficit. I don't know what that means.

Ms. TITUS. We do know he wants other people to step up and do their share, so that is kind of a hint what is coming.

Mr. SWAINE. Right. So gutting agencies, EPA and the State Department. And to me, it is just incredibly foolish if that is what is going to happen, because the State Department, more than any other agency, needs to have more funding. It has been operating on a shoestring for way too long. To put them at a lesser level of spending is going to make the ability of the United States to really be effective in places like the Far East, where it really counts, much, much less.

So I don't, in any way, sanction or endorse the kind of direction where the administration is going today. I think there has to be a clear, strategic assessment about what our long-term future is in the Western Pacific and how we bring to bear our most important assets—diplomatic, military, economic—to achieve those gains.

Much of U.S. policy has to do with process. Engagement is a process, as if it is something we can do or not do. We have no alternative to engaging with the Chinese. The Chinese are so big and so influential and the rest of the world is so committed to dealing with them that efforts by us to try and cut back on that would be totally self-destructive.

So we have to get smart about how we are going to be more engaged on this in a very changing dynamic for power relations, particularly in the Western Pacific. That is the only real area where the United States and China, in my view, can have serious problems. It is not over larger questions globally; it is primarily in the Western Pacific. And if we don't get that right, things are going to affect many other areas. So I agree that we need to have greater capabilities on the diplomatic side and on the economic side.

Ms. TITUS. We have seen, visiting some new democracies, where China has moved in there very eagerly to build infrastructure. And if you start cutting back at the State Department, cutting back the small budget that is foreign aid, this can have repercussions beyond the South China Sea.

Mr. Cheng, or Dr. Auslin?

Mr. AUSLIN. Congresswoman, just on your last point, I agree. We don't do infrastructure. We do capacity building. So if you want judges or police, you come to us. You want a road, you want a school, a power plant, you go to China or Japan. We should be doing infrastructure.

We have spent decades, however—to get to your earlier point—we have spent decades stripping our capability of spreading a democratic message about our values and our society and our culture. USIA, U.S. Information Agency, was disestablished years ago and rolled into the State Department. The current cuts may be extreme, but they are part of a long trend under both Democratic and Republican administrations to make it harder for our diplomats to get our message out. We do need to turn that around. I believe in it, but it is only part of a solution.

And as much as we need to engage with China, we have to be realistic. A country that wants to cooperate or be cooperative will do so without our blandishments. We have to understand the limitations of that even as we pursue it, because it sends a message to others who want to emulate our ways. Thank you.

Ms. TITUS. I guess I am out of time. I am sorry. Thank you.

Mr. YOHO. Thank you.

We will go to Ms. Gabbard from the great State of Hawaii.

Ms. GABBARD. Thank you, Mr. Chairman.

Thank you, gentlemen, for being here and sharing your insights and thoughts.

No one has really talked about North Korea yet, and how the various courses of action that are being suggested here will impact the very direct threat that we face from North Korea, and the reality that any resolution to North Korea's situation will require the engagement and cooperation of China in that.

So I would love to just hear each of your thoughts on specifically how you suggest your suggested course of action will impact the threat we face from North Korea. Start with Dr. Cheng.

Mr. CHENG. Representative, frankly, I don't see any solution to North Korea, because the North Korean regime has associated itself with retaining its nuclear capability, and China has repeatedly demonstrated for pretty much the last 30 years it has no intention of solving the North Korean problem, particularly for the United States.

And the reality is that North Korea's nuclear weapons aren't aimed at China; they are aimed at Japan, South Korea, and the United States, which, from the Chinese perspective, is not a great solution, but not necessarily a particularly troubling one.

I will note, however, that the one time that anything was done that truly caught the North Korean regime's attention was when we should the down Banco Delta Asia by using the financial networks to force the Chinese, again, to make that choice, the millions of dollars that they gain from working with North Korea or the billions in dollars in financial flows that would otherwise occur. Unfortunately, after less than a year, we decided that those sanctions were too dangerous to continue and sustain against North Korea.

Ms. GABBARD. Thank you.

Mr. AUSLIN. Congresswoman, thank you. I would agree with my colleague. I would say, however, I would modify it slightly to say there are no good solutions to North Korea. There are lots of bad solutions to North Korea. And I agree entirely that we have to give up the fiction that China wants, in any way, to solve North Korea, certainly for our own purposes.

I would say, however, that given the increasing erratic nature of the Kim Jong-un regime, the assassination of his half-brother, who was protected by China just a few weeks ago in Malaysia, as well as the assassination in 2014 or 2013, of Jang Song-Thaek, who was Kim Jong-un's uncle, but, more importantly, China's main agent in North Korea, means that Beijing is as worried about their influence as we are worried about our lack of. And there may be opportunities out of pure self-interest, which is a fine thing, for the two of us to figure out ways of pressuring that regime, or at least talking more creatively about how to contain it.

At some point, by the way, we are going to have to decide when we declare it a nuclear power. It is a nuclear power. I understand that we do not want to shred the nonproliferation regime, but we are going to have to wake up to reality one day. Thank you.

Ms. GABBARD. Thank you.

Mr. SWAINE. Well, I agree with what Dean and Michael have said already, that this is not a problem with a solution. I mean, it is really trying to maximize, or optimize, a bad situation. Unfortunately, what drives this situation the most is the behavior of North Korea, which no country outside of North Korea, has real control over, including the Chinese.

I believe that the Chinese have moved in their position toward a greater degree of cooperation and support in dealing with North Korea. They certainly wouldn't fully endorse everything that the United States might want to see toward North Korea for a legitimate national security interest of their own, as well as other interests, which may not be as, from our perspective, as legitimate; but I do think that we have choices here.

We have a very—the policy thus far has not worked. So we need to think about a new way of addressing this issue. We can't simply regard the Chinese as being the panacea, that they are going to solve it, because they are not going to solve it. So we have to think about how we can work with the Chinese, the South Koreans, and the Japanese to deal with it.

We have two different paths that we can go. One of them is toward a greater degree of unified sanctions against North Korea, in the hope that the regime will collapse or give up its nuclear weapons. I think that is very unlikely. I think they are committed to these weapons, and they are not likely to give them up. And they are going to continue to move toward a deliverable ICBM capability with a nuclear warhead. And when they get close to that capability, the question is, what do we do about that?

And, in my view, the only thing that one can do is you have to make a choice between being—well, you can combine both. You can be extremely clear about the consequences of any use or threat of use of a nuclear weapon by North Korea, that it will involve the destruction of North Korea, and that this applies to threats to South Korea and to Japan, our allies for whom we have a nuclear umbrella.

And at the same time, however, I think we have to consider whether or not it is possible to develop a diplomatic strategy in which you address each of the concerns that the North Koreans have said that they have on their security front. Many people say this is all useless, because the North Koreans will ignore all this and continue to take advantage of it. But you can make the argument that the United States and the other powers have not fully tried to implement what you call an omnibus approach to North Korea, that would give them over a period of time in response to certain actions that they would take a certain level of benefits for them, economic and diplomatic.

And if they turn those things down, and you offered them all in good faith and the Chinese sign onto that, then the basis for the Chinese to continue to not cooperate in dealing with North Korea will be reduced, in my view.

Ms. GABBARD. Thank you. Thank you, gentlemen.

There are clearly no easy answers to the situation, but, Dr. Swaine, I would argue that the time to ask that question what will we do is now. And understand that as we look at these other issues, whether it be the South China Sea or other issues within the region, we can't operate in a silo with any of them, because of the ripple effects that will occur as we look at the various threats that exist there.

Thank you.

Mr. YOHO. Thank you. And they have called votes. We have got 10½ minutes.

I am going to turn this over to Mr. Connolly from Virginia.

Mr. CONNOLLY. Thank you, Mr. Chairman.

And I would urge—welcome our panelists—if we can all be concise, I would appreciate it, because we have to go vote.

What my concern is, at the very start of the new administration, we have seen, or we are seeing policies that contradict each other with respect to this region and China. So we rattle the cage with a call to the President of Taiwan. We announce a budget that is going to add $54 billion in defense spending and the purpose of which is for ship building, military aircraft, and establishing "a more robust presence in key international waterways and checkpoints," like the South China Sea, while saying we are going to fund that, but cutting back on the State Department and AID specifically.

Now, I was just in Sri Lanka. The Chinese, as you said, Dr. Auslin, are building everything. You know, ports, airports, roads, bridges, high-rises, sports stadiums, hospitals, they are building it. But we are financing democratization. We are providing real, in-depth assistance, both through IRI and NDI to help, frankly, democratize institutions in Sri Lanka, and it is working. But that is funded through the AID program.

Now, if we retrench in our foreign assistance and diplomatic posture in places like the Philippines, Vietnam, Burma, Sri Lanka, doesn't that create a vacuum for the Chinese? And before you answer, so that is one vacuum I am worried about, and one set of contradictions.

The other is, in the first week, we rip up TPP. And what is happening as we speak, Beijing has summoned a region-wide convocation to talk about a new trade agreement that has zero provisions on labor, on human rights, and on the environment. And I don't know, I am a simple soul, but that seems like we just contradicted ourselves and, frankly, handed an enormous victory to the Chinese that will be very long-lasting.

Your comments?

Mr. CHENG. Representative, I believe that TPP was negotiated by the previous administration that indicated that it was not going to bring it forward to Congress. It was not going to present it for a vote at all. And in counting noses over who would have voted, I am not sure how many members of the previous administration's party could be relied upon to vote for TPP.

Mr. CONNOLLY. Irrelevant point, Mr. Cheng. I am making a different point. And by the way, I happen to be one of those people who would have and did.

However, what I am making—and if you don't want to answer it, then I will move to Dr. Auslin and Dr. Swaine. The question is, are we not handing an enormous victory, irrespective of what Obama's administration was prepared to do or not do—they were prepared to bring it to a vote, but time kind of ran out. But did we just hand the Chinese an enormous victory, and isn't the witness of that what is happening as we speak in Beijing?

Thirty percent of all of the world's economic activity is going to be covered by the agreement they are now forging, and I might add, U.S. allies, like Australia and New Zealand—maybe Australia isn't an ally anymore after the tongue-lashing they got from the new President.

Dr. Auslin, did you want to comment?

Mr. AUSLIN. Congressman, I would prefer to see the administration go back to TPP. However, if all we can get are bilaterals, then I think we should all push as strongly as possible to get bilaterals, starting with Japan.

Your point about the AID vacuum, I think, is important. It is an important part of our strategy. I would prefer to see that part of the budget increased as well. But we have to do a lot better at the messaging that we send out. We have not been very good under either Democratic or Republican administrations in the State Department sending out those messages.

Mr. CONNOLLY. Thank you.

Dr. Swaine, real quickly, because we are running out of time.

Mr. SWAINE. I basically agree with that, but I think the United States does really have to have a much better job, do a much better job of presenting what the economic costs and benefits are and what the advantages the United States gets from multilateral trade agreements, but it is just not in the position of doing that. Mr.

CONNOLLY. I just have never seen the United States quite so blatantly, in the matter of 1 month, contradict itself so pro- foundly with respect to something so important, namely, our rela- tions with China. So on the one hand, we want to deter them and we are going to build up military forces to do that; and on the other, we are going to unilaterally disarm on trade and foreign aid and diplomacy, because we are going to defund it.

I yield back. Thank you, Mr. Chairman.

Mr. YOHO. Thank you, gentlemen, for being here. Just kind of one last comment, because, again, what I hope to get out of this is to get enough information that we can help direct some of the foreign policies.

I read an article, and I got chastised for this because I brought it up in this committee. They were talking about how China, as you brought up, Dr. Auslin, how they go in and they build infrastructure, and we focus on other things. I think it is a misstep of ours. We should go in and build strong infrastructures and develop strong trading partners, and in that process we will bring people to our side and meet the goals that we have as far as human rights and things like that. And I think we should focus on that.

I want to point out to Dr. Swaine, and I know you are well aware of this. Robert Gates' book Duty, there was a section in there where they were talking about military sales to Taiwan. And a couple years ago, the Chinese negotiator raised holy Cain, because of the military sales. And our negotiator says, why are you making a big fuss over this? We have done this for many years, since 1979. He goes, yes, you did, but we were weak then; we are strong now. I think we are seeing that presence. So I think it is imperative that we come to an agreement of what we can do and can't do and forge those strong relationships.

I am going to turn this over to the ranking member, and let him finish, and we have to go vote.

Mr. SHERMAN. China will become more nationalistic as it needs to satisfy its own population, and even more nationalistic if they face economic reversals. TPP enshrined the idea that currency manipulation isn't a problem. And its rules of origin provision gave China a chance to have free access to the U.S. market on goods that were to be purportedly only 50 percent made in China, but, as an old accountant, I know that would be 80 or 90 percent. So 90 percent of the advantages of a free trade agreement. But at least they would have a made in Vietnam label put on.

We do not have—we will not put tariffs on China, because Wall Street won't let us. We will, instead, spend $50 billion extra on our military, because the Pentagon will want that; and we will meet the domestic needs of the institutions that are most powerful in our society. Wall Street will be happy. The Pentagon will be happy. Beijing will fan nationalism. And Ohio and Western Pennsylvania will suffer.

I yield back.

Mr. YOHO. Thank you for your comments.

Gentlemen, thank you for being here with your great information as you have helped us cipher through some things, and I look forward to dealing with you more. We have to go vote now. This meeting is adjourned, and thank you.

[Whereupon, at 3:57 p.m., the subcommittee was adjourned.]

A P P E N D I X

Material Submitted for the Record

SUBCOMMITTEE HEARING NOTICE
COMMITTEE ON FOREIGN AFFAIRS
U.S. HOUSE OF REPRESENTATIVES
WASHINGTON, DC 20515-6128

Subcommittee on Asia and the Pacific
Ted Yoho (R-FL), Chairman

February 28, 2017

TO: MEMBERS OF THE COMMITTEE ON FOREIGN AFFAIRS

You are respectfully requested to attend an OPEN hearing of the Committee on Foreign Affairs, to be held by the Subcommittee on Asia and the Pacific in Room 2172 of the Rayburn House Office Building (and available live on the Committee website at http://www.ForeignAffairs.house.gov):

DATE: Tuesday, February 28, 2017

TIME: 2:00 p.m.

SUBJECT: Checking China's Maritime Push

WITNESSES: Mr. Dean Cheng
                    Senior Research Fellow
                    Asian Studies Center
                    The Heritage Foundation

                    Michael Auslin, Ph.D.
                    Resident Scholar
                    Director of Japan Studies
                    American Enterprise Institute

                    Michael D. Swaine, Ph.D.
                    Senior Fellow
                    Asia Program
                    Carnegie Endowment for International Peace

By Direction of the Chairman

The Committee on Foreign Affairs seeks to make its facilities accessible to persons with disabilities. If you are in need of special accommodations, please call 202/225-5021 at least four business days in advance of the event, whenever practicable. Questions with regard to special accommodations in general (including availability of Committee materials in alternative formats and assistive listening devices) may be directed to the Committee.

COMMITTEE ON FOREIGN AFFAIRS

MINUTES OF SUBCOMMITTEE ON _____ *Asia and the Pacific* _____ HEARING

Day___*Tuesday*___Date___*February 28, 2017*___Room___*RHOB 2172*___

Starting Time___*2:28pm*___**Ending Time**___*3:55pm*___.

Recesses [_____] (____to____) (____to____) (____to____) (____to____) (____to____) (____to____)

Presiding Member(s)
Rep. Ted Yoho (R-FL)

Check all of the following that apply:

Open Session ☑
Executive (closed) Session ☐
Televised ☐

Electronically Recorded (taped) ☐
Stenographic Record ☐

TITLE OF HEARING:

"Checking China's Maritime Push"

SUBCOMMITTEE MEMBERS PRESENT:

Yoho, Kinzinger, Rohrabacher, Perry
Sherman, Bera, Titus, Deutch, Gabbard, Connolly

NON-SUBCOMMITTEE MEMBERS PRESENT: *(Mark with an * if they are not members of full committee.)*

N/A

HEARING WITNESSES: Same as meeting notice attached? Yes ☑ No ☐
(If "no", please list below and include title, agency, department, or organization.)

STATEMENTS FOR THE RECORD: *(List any statements submitted for the record.)*

Wagner

TIME SCHEDULED TO RECONVENE _____
or
TIME ADJOURNED ___*3:55pm*___

Subcommittee Staff Associate

58

Statement and Questions for the Record
Congresswoman Ann Wagner
AP Subcommittee Hearing: "Checking China's Maritime Push"
February 28, 2017

Thank you, Mr. Chairman, for holding this hearing. Last month, along with my colleague Congressman Castro, I founded the Congressional Caucus on ASEAN. Ensuring that Southeast Asian interests are heard loud and clear in the maritime discussion is an important dimension to this challenge.

1. Mr. Auslin, can you please discuss progress in the Japan-ASEAN defense initiative on maritime security cooperation? How do you hope the defense initiative will evolve?
2. Japan recently decided to transfer or donate defense equipment to the Philippines and Vietnam. Mr. Auslin, how will improved naval capacity in ASEAN help Southeast Asia better respond to gray zone situations before they escalate?
3. Mr. Swaine, or others, the growing U.S.-India naval partnership includes information-sharing about Chinese maritime action in the Indian Ocean. Can you discuss New Delhi's concerns with Chinese action in the Indian Ocean?

Cheng: Various Indian officials, academics, and analysts have expressed concerns about China's growing presence in the Indian Ocean region. There have been longstanding fears that Chinese investments across the region, sometimes characterized as the "string of pearls," are laying the foundation for future expansion of China's military presence. China has established a military base in Djibouti, and has deployed submarines to the Indian Ocean, in addition to supporting a regular presence in the Gulf of Aden.

For Indian defense planners, the situation is further complicated by the close relationship between China and Pakistan. Indian defense planners have to worry that, in the event of a conflict with Pakistan, China will support India, not only politically, but possibly through provision of intelligence and other assistance.

Swaine: New Delhi's security concerns toward China center on the fear that a larger, more capable Chinese navy will possess the ability to control or dominate India's southern maritime region and thus both reduce Indian security and limit India's efforts to expand its influence beyond the region into East Asia and possibly the Middle East. A strong Chinese naval presence in the Indian Ocean could also put pressure on India during a possible future confrontation with China over territorial or other disputes along India's northern border with Beijing. Hence, while Sino-Indian diplomatic and economic relations are generally cordial, New Delhi nonetheless wants to keep a close watch on Chinese activities in the Indian Ocean and if possible counter-balance China's growing capabilities there. Think of this as Indian hedging.

4. Last year, former Taiwanese president Lee Teng-hui wrote that the Senkaku islands belong to Japan. In response, then-KMT President Ma Ying-jeou and DPP President-elect Tsai Ing-wen insisted that the Senkaku islands belong to Taiwan. Mr. Cheng, are Lee's remarks at all indicative of a future shift in Taiwan's approach to the territorial dispute?

Cheng: Taiwan, like the PRC, has never renounced its claim to the Senkakus (which they term the Diaoyutai islands). The position enunciated by former Taiwanese president Lee is therefore not that of the government in Taipei, or either major political party.

Former President Lee's comments should be seen in the context of his background, which included growing up on Taiwan when it was still a Japanese colony, and included volunteering to serve in the Imperial Japanese armed forces during World War II. In 2015, he was heavily criticized for referring to Japan as "the motherland."[1]

---

[1] "Ex-President Lee Teng-hui Under Fire for Calling Japan 'the Motherland,'" South China Morning Post (August 21, 2015). http://www.scmp.com/news/china/policies-politics/article/1851501/ex-taiwan-president-lee-under-fire-calling-japan